Cai

L

HarperCollins*Publishers*

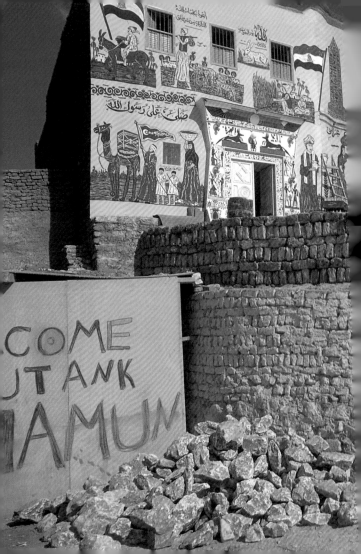

This book was produced using QuarkXPress™ and
Adobe Illustrator 88™ on Apple Macintosh™ computers
and output to separated film on a Linotronic™ 300 Imagesetter

Text: Delia Pemberton
Photography: Christine Osborne
Electronic Cartography: Susan Harvey Design
Design: Ted Carden

First published 1991
Copyright © HarperCollins Publishers
Printed in Hong Kong
ISBN 0 00 435764-7

HOW TO USE THIS BOOK

Your Collins Traveller Guide will help you find your way around your holiday destination quickly and easily. It is split into two sections which are colour-coded:

The blue section provides you with an alphabetical sequence of headings, from **ART GALLERIES** to **WALKS**, for both Cairo and Luxor. Each entry within a topic includes information on how to get there, when it will be open and what to expect. Furthermore, every page has its own map showing the position of each item and the nearest landmark. This allows you to orientate yourself quickly and easily in your new surroundings.

To find what you want to do – having dinner, visiting a museum, going for a walk or shopping for gifts – simply flick through the blue headings and take your pick!

The red section is an alphabetical list of information providing essential facts about places and cultural items – 'What is a madrasa?', 'When is the Cairo International Film Festival?', 'Where is Aswan?' – and expanding on subjects touched on in the first half of the book. This section also contains practical travel information. It ranges through how to find accommodation, where to hire a car, the variety of eating places and food available, tips on health, information on money, which news-papers are available, how to find a taxi and where the youth hostels are. It is lively and informative and easy to use. Each band shows the first three letters of the first entry on the page. Simply flick through the bands till you find the entry you need!

All the main entries are also cross-referenced to help you find them. Names in small capitals – **CAIRO-CHILDREN** – tell you that there is more information about the item you are looking for under the topic on chil-dren in the first part of the book. So when you read 'see **CAIRO-CHIL-DREN**' you turn to the blue heading for **CAIRO-CHILDREN**. The instruction 'see **A-Z**' after a word lets you know that the word has its own entry in the second part of the book. Words in bold type – **Monasteries** – also let you know that there is an entry in the A-Z for the indicated name. In both cases just look under the appropriate heading in the red section. Packed full of information and easy to use – you'll always know where you are with your Collins Traveller Guide!

EGYPTIAN CENTER
FOR INTERNATIONAL
CULTURAL
COOPERATION

Nile

Corniche el Nil

Sabti

26 July St

AKHNA

Nile St

Gezira St

26 July S

GALLERY
MERVET
MASOUD

EL SALAAM
GALLERY

6 October Bridge

Tahrir St

Tahrir St

Dokki St

Tahrir St

EL NIL
EXHIBITION
HALL

Kasr el Aini

El Gam'a
Bridge

Giza St

Nile

Manial St

Roda St

AIDA
GALLERY

Nile St

Corniche el Nil

Abu Selyne St

Huna el Qahira – 'This is Cairo' – announces the radio, and a snatch of patriotic music bursts onto the city air to mingle with the blare of motor horns, the shouts of fruit sellers and the sobbing love songs issuing from ghetto blasters. At three o'clock, Cairo simmers in the afternoon heat. Traffic, anticipating the evening rush still an hour away, flows like treacle; the pavements are a mass of seething humanity. Seeming perpetually on the verge of bursting, Cairo nonetheless somehow makes room for almost another million

INTRODUCTION

new inhabitants every year. Suddenly the traffic grinds to a halt and a whirling cloud of dust appears, at its centre a herd of camels in full gallop. A brief glimpse of the drivers – dark Nubians in white robes and turbans, like desert princes – and the vision is gone: Cairo is a city that likes to keep the visitor off balance. The traffic crawls on; itinerant vendors move between the cars proffering boxes of tissues, strings of jasmine flowers, velvet cushions. A tide of pedestrians surges past – stu-

dents with armfuls of books, sleek businessmen in suits and expensive aftershave, countrywomen in black shawls, teenagers in jeans and T-shirts, farmers in long *galabeyas* and brown felt caps. A boy on a bicycle weaves between the cars, holding a live kid round his neck with one hand and steering with the other. An entire family on a scooter – the wife primly seated side-saddle – squeezes past a bus with clinging youths dangling from its doors and windows. And in the distance, beyond the sprawl of dusty beige tower blocks, the Pyramids stand aloof on the desert horizon. The coachloads of tourists, the camels, the scarab-vendors and the Coca-Cola stands are all invisible from here: only the three monumental forms shimmer through the haze – the silent, inscrutable guardians of Egypt's 5000 years of history.

Awed by its great antiquity, the medieval Arabs spoke of Cairo as the 'Mother of the World', yet the city's origins belong not to the Pharaonic period but to the Christian era. As early as the 1stC AD, the revolutionary new faith found a natural home in the land whose most ancient beliefs were

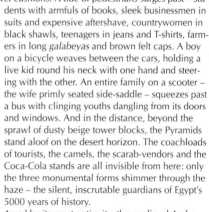

founded on the concept of life after death; in time, a flourishing community grew up around the Roman Fortress of Babylon, in the area now known as Old Cairo. Today Egypt's Christians, the Copts, only account for 10% of the country's population, but the churches and monasteries of Old Cairo and the Wadi Natrun are the fascinating legacy of what was once the principal faith of Egypt.

Following the Arab conquest in the 7thC, a new settlement was established at Fustat, close to Old Cairo, but it was the 10thC Fatimids who relocated the city and named it El Qahira (Cairo) after the warlike planet Mars (El Qahir) which was in the ascendant at the time. They also founded El Azhar, the world's first university, establishing Cairo as the intellectual and theological centre of the Arab world for centuries to come. Much of medieval Cairo survives: enter by one of the great city gates through which Saracen armies marched forth to do battle with Crusaders, and where later the first European traders arrived to do business. Stand in an old caravanserai, where bales of silks and spices were unloaded while merchants swapped stories of distant lands. Wander the maze of narrow streets, sidestepping donkeys, past shops where coppersmiths and weavers ply their ancient trades in an atmosphere pungent with the scents of incense, dung and frying onions. Pause at a café to sip a tiny, bitter coffee amid the slap of backgammon

pieces, the shouts of waiters and the soft gurgle of water pipes. Take a look behind those huge studded doors in the high blank walls to discover hidden palaces with green, shady gardens, or peaceful mosques hallowed by centuries of prayer.

For many centuries Islam has been the major inspiration behind Cairo's architecture, and succeeding generations of rulers from the Fatimids and Ayyubids to the Mamluks and Ottomans continued to enrich its wealth of religious monuments until it truly became the fabled 'City of a Thousand Minarets'. And from those minarets, five times daily, the call to prayer echoes across the rooftops: 'God is great . . . There is no God but God.' Serene, unchanging, the muezzin's cry is like a refrain permeating the city's consciousness, punctuating the day, marking off the months, the years, the centuries.

Egypt's great antiquity is inescapable. If after visiting the ruins of Memphis and Sakkara, the Pyramids and Sphinx at Giza, and monuments of Christian and Islamic Cairo confusion sets in, where better to head for elucidation than one of the city's excellent museums – the Egyptian Museum, Coptic Museum and Museum of Islamic Art are all 'musts'. Even children can find history fun on a visit to the Pharaonic Village, where they can sail around living tableaux of Ancient Egyptian life and dress up as pharaohs! More bloodthirsty nippers will probably enjoy Saladin's Citadel, where they can investigate the medieval dungeons before inspecting a horribly comprehensive array of weaponry in the Military Museum. Alternatively, a ride to the top of the Cairo Tower

may do the trick – kids and adults alike find the panoramic view fascinating. Look out for some of the city's 20thC landmarks, such as the new Opera House, for Cairo is also one of the most modern of cities, with a thriving cultural life, stylish couturiers and first-class restaurants and nightspots. Yet still at its heart, the Nile continues to flow as it has for millennia, a river of many moods – misty and mysterious at dawn, by day bustling with river traffic and at night silent and sparkling with the reflections of the city's lights.

Nearly 700 km upstream, at Luxor, the Nile seems a different river altogether when set against a backdrop of pink limestone cliffs and green fields. In place of Cairo's barges and river buses, graceful white-sailed feluccas skim the water, and stately Nile cruisers manoeuvre and dock at the quays in front of Luxor Temple, where picturesque horse carriages clop and jingle along the tree-lined Corniche. There were quays here in ancient times, too, when 'Hundred-gated Thebes' was Egypt's capital, but these were for the sacred boats which carried the gods' images on their river processions from Karnak. The religious heart of the ancient kingdom, Karnak's acres of ruined temples are like a directory of ancient Egyptian architecture, with scattered capitals, obelisks and sphinxes. Its massive pylon towers over the surrounding countryside, mute but powerful testimony to the authority once vested in the priests of Amun.

For many visitors, the monuments of the Theban West Bank – the great royal mortuary temples, the Tombs of the Nobles, the Valley of the Kings and Valley of the Queens – are Egypt's chief attraction. Few expect to see the lively paintings of ancient agricultural practices duplicated by modern farmers in the surrounding fields, but just as parts of Cairo have remained in the Middle Ages, so Luxor's countryside recalls the time of the pharaohs. And at sunset, when the sun's great red disc sinks below the horizon like the god Re entering the Underworld, and the call to prayer issues from the mosques, time scarcely seems to exist at all: there is only the Nile, and Egypt, eternal.

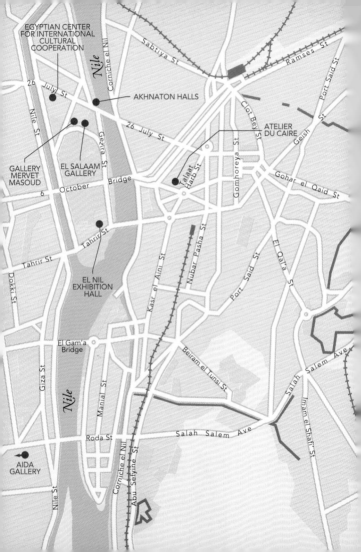

AIDA GALLERY Sakkara Rd, 6 km from Pyramids Rd, Pyramids.
❏ Closed Fri.
The gallery houses the work of famous Egyptian artists, plus a permanent display of furniture.

AKHNATON HALLS Zamalek Arts Center, 1 Mahad el Swisry St, Zamalek. Opposite the Cairo Marriott Hotel.
❏ Closed Fri.
Four galleries housing exhibitions ranging from avant-garde Egyptian painting to visiting shows of well-known European artists.

ATELIER DU CAIRE 2 Karim el Dawla St, Central Cairo. Near Talaat Harb Sq.
❏ Daily.
Artists' cooperative; two galleries displaying contemporary art. The small café is a good place to mingle with creative types.

EGYPTIAN CENTER FOR INTERNATIONAL CULTURAL COOPERATION 11 Shagarat el Durr St, Zamalek.
❏ Closed Fri.
Fine arts and crafts, plus cultural events.

GALLERY MERVET MASOUD 6 Gezira St, Zamalek.
❏ Closed Sun.
A gallery displaying the fine arts and antique furniture.

EL NIL EXHIBITION HALL Gezira Exhibition Grounds, Tahrir St, Gezira. Near Galaa Bridge.
❏ Closed Fri.
Large, modern public gallery housing important shows such as the Cairo Biennale.

EL SALAAM GALLERY 1 Sheikh el Marsafi St, Zamalek, in basement of the Mahmud Khalil Museum. Behind the Cairo Marriott Hotel.
❏ Daily.
Contemporary fine arts and crafts. See **CAIRO-MUSEUMS 2**.

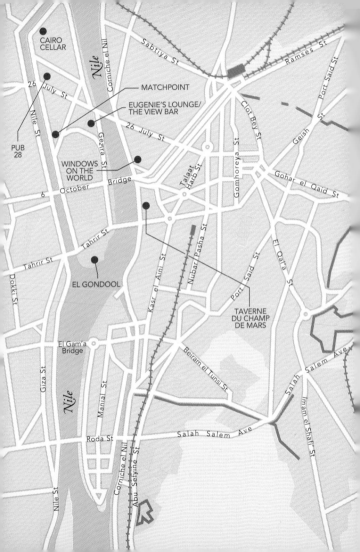

CAIRO
CELLAR

Nile

Sabtiya St

Comiche el Nil

Ramses St

26 July St

MATCHPOINT

EUGENIE'S LOUNGE/
THE VIEW BAR

Nile St

26 July St

Gezira St

PUB
28

WINDOWS
ON THE
WORLD

6 October

Bridge

Talaat
Harb St

Gomhoreya St

Clot Bey St

Geish St

Port Said St

Gohar el Qaid St

Tahrir St

Tahrir St

Tahrir St

Dokki St

EL GONDOOL

Kasr el Aini St

Nubar Pasha St

Port Said St

El Qala'a St

TAVERNE
DU CHAMP
DE MARS

Giza St

El Gam'a
Bridge

Manial St

Beiram el Tunsi St

Salah Salem Ave

Roda St

Nile

Coriche el Nil

Abu Seriyne St

Salah Salem Ave

Salah Salem Ave

Imam el Shafi' St

Bars

CAIRO CELLAR President Hotel, 22 Taha Hussein St, Zamalek.
❑ 1200-0200.
Popular cellar bar which also serves excellent mezze.

EUGENIE'S LOUNGE Cairo Marriott Hotel, Gezira Palace,
Zamalek.
❑ 1100-0200.
Cocktails and live music in the elegant surroundings of the 19thC Gezira Palace (see **CAIRO-BUILDINGS & MONUMENTS 3***).*

EL GONDOOL El Gezira Sheraton, Tahrir Gardens, Gezira.
❑ 1100-0200.
Plush cocktail bar with live music and views of the Nile Fountain.

MATCHPOINT Four Corners, 4 Hassan Sabry St, Zamalek.
❑1300-0100. ❑ Min. charge.
Snacks, drinks and pub games in a lively and noisy atmosphere.

PUB 28 28 Shagarat el Durr St, Zamalek.
❑ 1200-0100.
English-style pub with restaurant.

TAVERNE DU CHAMP DE MARS Nile Hilton Hotel, Corniche
el Nil, Central Cairo.
❑ 1100-0200.
Pub-style bar serving snacks and a daily buffet. Live music.

THE VIEW BAR Cairo Marriott Hotel, Gezira Palace, Zamalek.
❑ 1700-0200.
20th-floor bar with spectacular view.

WINDOWS ON THE WORLD Ramses Hilton Hotel, Corniche el
Nil, Central Cairo.
❑ 1600-0200.
Glamorous 36th-floor bar with huge windows offering a breathtaking panoramic view of Cairo by night. Live music.

*Archaeological sites are generally open 0600-1800 summer, 0600-1600 winter. During Ramadan (see **A-Z**) sites open later and close earlier.*

PYRAMIDS & SPHINX Giza Plateau, Pyramids.
One of the Seven Wonders of the Ancient World, the Pyramids and Sphinx are rightly on every traveller's itinerary. See **CAIRO-WALK 1**, **A-Z**.

BEN EZRA SYNAGOGUE Old Cairo.
Claimed to be Cairo's oldest synagogue, the present building dates from the 12thC; restorations currently in progress aim to recover its past opulence. See **CAIRO-WALK 2**, **A-Z**.

EL MU'ALLAQA CHURCH Old Cairo.
*Known as the Hanging Church (see **A-Z**), it is constructed over the gates of the Fortress of Babylon (see below). The inlaid woodwork on the screen is particularly fine. See* **CAIRO-WALK 2**.

FORTRESS OF BABYLON Old Cairo.
*2ndC Roman fortress marking the location of Cairo's first settlement, now the site of the Coptic Museum (see **A-Z**). See* **CAIRO-WALK 2**, **A-Z**.

MEMPHIS 43 km southwest of Cairo.
*The scattered remains of Egypt's Old Kingdom capital including fragments of temples, a fallen colossus of Ramesses II (see **A-Z**) and a marble sphinx. See* **CAIRO-EXCURSION 1**, **A-Z**.

SAKKARA 45 km southwest of Cairo.
*Once the necropolis of Memphis (see above), this extensive site includes the Step Pyramid complex and the Mastabas of the Nobles (see **A-Z**), as well as several late Old Kingdom pyramids and the Serapeum, where the mummies of sacred bulls were laid to rest. See* **CAIRO-EXCURSION 1**, **A-Z**.

ST. SERGIUS' CHURCH Old Cairo.
One of Cairo's oldest churches, its crypt incorporates a cave where the Holy Family is said to have stayed during the Flight into Egypt. See **CAIRO-WALK 2**, **A-Z**.

Buildings & Monuments 2

AQUEDUCT Old Cairo.
Over 3 km long, the Aqueduct dates from the Mamluk period; it continued to serve the city until the late 19thC. See **A-Z**.

EL AZHAR Azhar Sq. Near Khan el Khalili.
One of Cairo's first mosques, and the world's oldest university. See **A-Z**.

BAYT EL SUHAYMI Darb el Asfour. Near Khan el Khalili.
❑ 0900-1600 Sat.-Thu., 0900-1200, 1300-1600 Fri.
Beautifully restored house of the Ottoman period. See **A-Z**.

CITADEL
❑ 0900-1700.
Saladin's Citadel. See **CAIRO-MUSEUMS 1 & 2, WALK 3, A-Z**.

CITY OF THE DEAD
Cairo's great medieval cemeteries today accommodate the homes of the poor alongside the magnificent tombs of saints and sultans, notably that of Qaitbey, considered the jewel of Mamluk architecture. See **A-Z**.

CITY WALLS
Fatimid (see **A-Z***) city walls and gates. See* **A-Z**.

IBN TULUN MOSQUE Ahmed ibn Tulun Sq.
Cairo's oldest complete mosque, begun in the 9thC. See **A-Z**.

NILOMETER Roda Island.
The oldest Islamic monument in Cairo, the Nilometer once measured the height of the Nile's annual flood. See **A-Z**.

QALAWUN COMPLEX Mu'izz li Din Allah St.
13thC memorial complex of the Sultan Qalawun. See **A-Z**.

SULTAN HASSAN MADRASA El Qal'a St. Near the Citadel.
This 14thC madrasa (see **A-Z***) and mausoleum is one of the finest examples of Islamic architecture in Cairo. See* **A-Z**.

Nile

Sabtiya St

Corniche el Nil

GEZIRA
PALACE

Ramses St

Port Said St

SAKAKINI
PALACE

26 July St

Clot Bey St

26 July St

Geish St

Nile St

Gezira St

Gomhoreya St

Gohar el Qaid St

CAIRO
TOWER

6 October Bridge

Talaat Harb St

El Qala St

Tahrir St

Tahrir St

OPERA
HOUSE

Kasr el Aini St

Nubar Pasha St

Port Said St

Dokki St

MANIAL
PALACE

Salah Salem Ave

El Gam'a
Bridge

Beiram el Tunsi St

Salah Salem Ave

Imam el Shafi St

Giza St

Manial St

Nile

Roda St

Salah Salem Ave

Corniche el Nil

Abu Seljine St

Nile St

HARRANIA VILLAGE/
RENAISSANCE OF EGYPT

CAIRO TOWER Near Gezira Exhibition Grounds, Gezira.
❑ 0900-2400.
One of the landmarks of modern Cairo, offering a panoramic view over the city. See **A-Z**.

GEZIRA PALACE Cairo Marriott Hotel, Gezira Palace St, Zamalek.
❑ Unrestricted access.
Built by the Khedive Ismail to accommodate royalty attending the opening of the Suez Canal. Now houses public areas of the Marriott Hotel.

HARRANIA VILLAGE Sakkara Rd, Pyramids.
❑ 1000-1700.
Inspired by the work of the architect Wissa Wassef, the craft school located here has won the Aga Khan Architectural Award. See **CAIRO-EXCURSION 1**.

MANIAL PALACE Manial Palace St, Roda Island. Near University Bridge.
❑ 0900-1600.
Built in 1901, the several palace buildings display a curious blend of Eastern and Western styles. See **CAIRO-MUSEUMS 2**, **A-Z**.

OPERA HOUSE Gezira Exhibition Grounds, Tahrir St, Gezira. Near Galaa Bridge.
❑ Open during performances only.
Cairo's newest landmark, and a striking example of modern Arab architecture. See **A-Z**, **Theatre**.

RENAISSANCE OF EGYPT University Sq., Giza.
This monumental sculpture in pink granite, representing the rebirth of the Egyptian spirit, is the work of Mahmud Mukhtar (see **A-Z**).

SAKAKINI PALACE Sakakini Sq.
❑ 0900-1400 Sat.-Thu.
An elaborate rococo residence; built in 1898, it now houses the Museum of Hygiene and Medicine.

Nile

Sabtiya St

Ramses St

Corniche el Nil

26 July St

À L'AMERICAINE

Clot Bey St

Port Said St

GROPPI GARDEN

26 July St

Gomhoreya St

Geish St

GROPPI

Gezira St

Talaat Harb St

Gohar el Qaid St

FISHAWI/ NAGUIB MAHFOUZ

Nile St

6 October Bridge

CAFÉ RICHE

Tahrir St

Kasr el Aini St

Nubar Pasha St

Port Said St

El Qal'a St

Dokki St

Tahrir St

El Gam'a Bridge

Beiram el Tunsi St

Salah Salem Ave

Giza St

Manial St

Nile

Salah Salem Ave

Imam el Shafi'i St

Nile St

Roda St

Corniche el Nil

Abu Sefyne St

Salah Salem Ave

À L'AMERICAINE 7 26 July St & 44 Talaat Harb St, Central Cairo.
❏ 0700-2300.
Art Deco coffee shop popular with the legal profession.

CAFÉ RICHE 17 Talaat Harb St, Central Cairo.
❏ 0900-0100.
Once the meeting place of Egypt's leading intellectuals, this open-air street café carries a reputation for intrigue; the Egyptian Revolution is said to have been planned here. Hopefully the restorations currently in progress will not destroy its unique atmosphere.

FISHAWI Off Badestan Lane, Khan el Khalili.
❏ 24 hr.
Cairo's oldest café, in a narrow alleyway in the heart of the bazaar district, has been the ḥaunt of rich and poor, famous and infamous, for over two centuries. The décor includes chandeliers and mirrors: an absolute 'must'.

GROPPI Talaat Harb Sq., Central Cairo.
❏ 0730-2200.
Worth a visit for its magnificent Art Deco mosaic entrance alone, this once-famous café is still atmospheric, and boasts a takeaway delicatessen and patisserie.

GROPPI GARDEN 46 Abdel Khalek Sarwat St, Central Cairo.
❏ 0730-2100.
A welcome oasis away from the hustle and bustle of the city centre, this pleasant garden café was a favourite with British troops during World War II.

NAGUIB MAHFOUZ Badestan Lane, Khan el Khalili.
❏ 1000-2200.
An elegant new café run by the Oberoi hotel chain in the heart of the bazaar area and named after Egypt's Nobel prize-winning author who came from this district. The perfect place to rest and watch the world go by while sipping a mint tea.

Children

AQUARIUM Gezira St, Zamalek.
❑ 0830-1600.
Large park with moonscape grottoes housing fish tanks.

DR RAGAB'S PHARAONIC VILLAGE Jacob Island, Sakiet
Miky, Giza. Access by boat from Bahr el Aazam, Nile St, Giza.
❑ 0900-1600.
*Sail around living tableaux of ancient Egyptian life, and have your photo
taken in Pharaonic dress! Restaurant and playground.*

EGYPTIAN NATIONAL CIRCUS Nile St, Agouza, tel: 3464870.
❑ Nightly at 2130. Shows last approximately 2 hr 30 min.
Traditional circus featuring clowns, animals, acrobats and trapeze artists.

EL SALAM HOTEL Abdel Hamid Badawi St, Heliopolis.
Tel: 2455155.
English-language films for children on Fri. am; telephone for details.

FELFELA VILLAGE Mariotia Canal, Pyramids.
❑ 1000-1800.
*Restaurant with mini-funfair, menagerie and tableaux of Egyptian village
life. Weekend family shows include folk dancing and performing horses.*

KOOKY PARK Mansuriya St, Pyramids. Behind Jolie Ville Hotel.
❑ 1500-2400.
*Amusement park offering various rides including a ghost train, shooting
gallery, pony rides and a restaurant.*

MERRYLAND PARK Hegaz St, Roxy, Heliopolis.
❑ 0900-1700.
Park with a playground, mini-zoo and a lake for boat rides.

ZOO Giza St, Dokki.
❑ 0900-1700.
*Founded in 1890, a traditional zoo extending over 52 acres. Facilities
include restaurants, picnic areas and pony rides. See **A-Z**.*

Crafts

COPPERSMITHS' BAZAAR Suq el Nahhaseen. Near Khan el Khalili.
The traditional coppersmiths' street where numerous small factories turn out brass and copper trays, lamps and vessels.

GOLDSMITHS' BAZAAR Suq el Sagha. Near Khan el Khalili.
The ancient jewellers' quarter; some of the shops here were established over 200 years ago. An interesting sight is the piercing of beads with a bow drill – a technique in use since Pharaonic times.

MUSAFIRKHANA PALACE Darb el Tablawi, tel: 920472.
A beautiful 18thC palace now housing artists' studios. See **A-Z**.

NADIM (National Art Development Institute of Mashrabia), El Masanea St, Dokki. South of the Coca-Cola Bottling Co.
❑ 1100-1300 Mon.-Sat., or by appointment, tel: 715927.
Dedicated to preserving the techniques and standards of Cairo's rich woodworking heritage, Nadim can produce and supply anything made in carved, inlaid or turned wood.

TENTMAKERS' BAZAAR Suq el Khayamia. Near Bab Zuwayla.
The last of Cairo's ancient covered bazaars houses tiny shops where men sew the colourful appliqué fabrics once used for festive marquees and now adapted for use as cushion covers, bedspreads and wall hangings.

WIKALAT EL GHURI Near Khan el Khalili.
❑ 1000-1400 Sun.-Thu. ❑ Admission fee.
A recently restored medieval caravanserai now housing studios for craftsmen in various disciplines, including stained glass. See **A-Z**.

WISSA WASSEF SCHOOL Sakkara Rd, Harrania.
❑ 1000-1700; workshops closed Fri.
World-famous school for tapestries and pottery started by the architect Ramses Wissa Wassef. The complex received the Aga Khan Award for its architecture. There is a museum of Wissa Wassef tapestries, and work is also for sale. See **A-Z**.

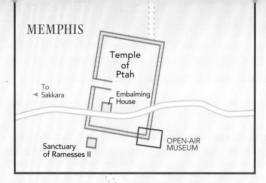

MEMPHIS

Temple of Ptah

To Sakkara

Embalming House

OPEN-AIR MUSEUM

Sanctuary of Ramesses II

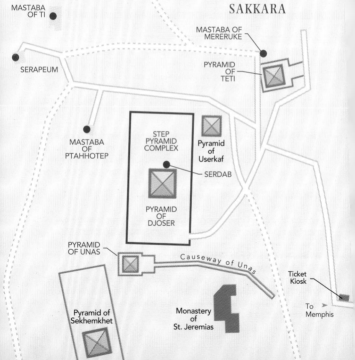

SAKKARA

MASTABA OF TI

MASTABA OF MERERUKE

SERAPEUM

PYRAMID OF TETI

MASTABA OF PTAHHOTEP

STEP PYRAMID COMPLEX

Pyramid of Userkaf

SERDAB

PYRAMID OF DJOSER

PYRAMID OF UNAS

Causeway of Unas

Ticket Kiosk

To Memphis

Pyramid of Sekhemkhet

Monastery of St. Jeremias

Excursion 1

*By road 45 km southwest to Memphis and Sakkara. Organized
excursions are also available.*

Situated close to the junction of the Nile Valley and the Delta,
Memphis (see **A-Z**) became the first capital of the newly-united Egypt
around 3200 BC. Today, few of the city's remains are recognizable;
there is, however, an interesting open-air museum where pride of place
is given to a fallen limestone colossus of Ramesses II (see **A-Z**).
One of the most important archaeological sites in Egypt, Sakkara (see
A-Z) – the necropolis of Memphis – has funerary remains spanning over
3000 years. The best known is the Step Pyramid complex, built for the
pharaoh Djoser around 2700 BC. Designed by the legendary Imhotep, it
is the world's oldest stone monument and comprises halls, shrines and
courts as well as the pyramid itself. An interesting feature of the architecture is that many of the structures imitate organic prototypes such as
picket fences and log ceilings. Behind the pyramid is the serdab, a special hidden chamber designed to house the king's statue. (The figure
now *in situ* is a replica, the original being in the Egyptian Museum.)
Well worth visiting also are the Mastabas of the Nobles (see **A-Z**), most
of which date from the Fifth and Sixth Dynasties. Containing suites of
up to 30 rooms, they are best known for their fine limestone reliefs with
scenes of offerings and daily activities, all intended to ensure an after-
life in the style to which the deceased had become accustomed. The
tombs' most important room was the burial chapel, which was always
equipped with a false door to enable the passage of the departed's spirit. Among the best are those belonging to Ti, Ptahhotep and Mereruke.
The pyramids of Unas and Teti also date from this period; resembling
large heaps of rubble from the outside, the subterranean chambers
boast fine hieroglyphic inscriptions. Finally, be sure to visit the
Serapeum, an extraordinary underground gallery where the mummies
of sacred Apis bulls were laid to rest in massive stone sarcophagi.
Returning to Cairo along the Sakkara Rd, stop at Harrania (see **CAIRO-
BUILDINGS & MONUMENTS 3**) to visit the Wissa Wassef School (see **A-Z**).
Started by the pioneering architect Ramses Wissa Wassef, the school
has won an Aga Khan Award for its architecture. It includes tapestry
and batik workshops, a pottery studio and a museum.

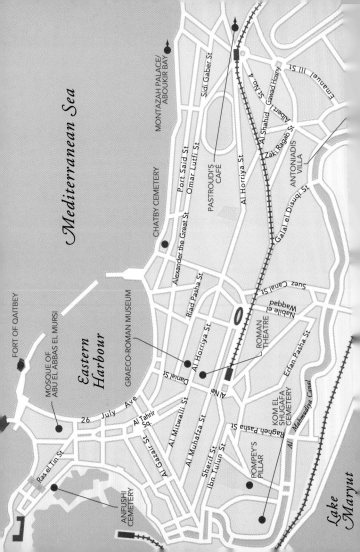

*By road or rail 225 km north to Alexandria (see **A-Z**). Organized excursions are also available.*

Planned by Alexander the Great (see **A-Z**), Alexandria came to fame as Egypt's capital under the Ptolemies and Romans. During its Golden Age it was home to the most eminent artists and scientists, and cradle of the Neo-Platonist school of philosophy presided over by the female philosopher Hypatia.

Today, however, many of its most famous ancient buildings, such as the Library, the Museum and the Pharos – the lighthouse which was one of the Seven Wonders of the World – are lost forever, but there is still much which makes a day excursion from Cairo worthwhile. Cemeteries at Chatby, Anfushi and Kom el Shugafa have interesting examples of Graeco-Roman tombs, including underground catacombs. The Roman Theatre at Kom el Dik and Pompey's Pillar (actually erected in honour of the Emperor Diocletian) are also worth seeing. For the best impression of life (and death) in ancient Alexandria, you must go to the Graeco-Roman Museum with its impressive collections of statuary, tomb paintings and funerary equipment.

Islamic monuments include the 15thC fort of Qaitbey, and the fine 18thC mosque of Abu el Abbas el Mursi. It is also pleasant to savour the city's more recent cosmopolitan inheritance, immortalized in the works of E. M. Forster and Lawrence Durrell. A new museum in the Greek consulate at 63 Alexander the Great St is dedicated to the work of the 'old poet of the city', C. P. Cavafy. To recapture the flavour of those times, wander the fine old boulevards, sip a coffee at Pastroudi's, 39 Abdel Nasser Ave, or visit the Antoniadis Villa, once owned by a wealthy Greek family. The gardens of Montazah Palace, once a royal residence, make a good picnic spot. Further east is Aboukir Bay, where Nelson's British fleet won a notable victory against Napoleon (see **A-Z**) in 1798. The sea has always been closely linked to Alexandria's fortune, and today, besides serving as a port, the city is best known for its beaches where millions of Cairenes flock during the summer.

Finally, after a day's sightseeing, no visitor should leave Alexandria without trying one of the famous seafood restaurants where the freshest of fish, shrimp or lobster is cooked to the customer's requirements.

THE FAYYUM

Lake Karun

To Cairo

KOM USHIM (KARANIS)

MEIDUM PYRAMID

HAWARA PYRAMID

LAHUN PYRAMID

MEDINET FAYYUM

FIDIMIN

SILIYIN

DIONYSIAS

Excursion 3

By road 70 km to the Fayyum. Organized excursions are also available.

The Fayyum (see **A-Z**) is a large semi-oasis area to the southwest of Cairo; it is accessible either by the desert road from the Pyramids or via Beni Suef on the Nile. It is a popular weekend retreat for Cairenes seeking escape from the heat and dust of the city, especially during the spring festival of Shamm el Nissim.

Watered both by artesian springs and by a branch of the Nile called the Bahr Yusef, the Fayyum is a predominantly agricultural area and a centre for market gardening. A drive through its cultivated areas is a wonderful opportunity to see all kinds of exotic produce growing. Look out for mango, bananas, melons and prickly pears. Also typical of the Fayyum are the fanciful crenellated pigeon houses built of white-washed earthenware pots; the birds are kept both for their meat and for the useful guano.

At the heart of the Fayyum is the town of Medinet Fayyum where you can sit in the open-air café drinking tea and listening to the creaking music of the old wooden water wheels. The nearby market is a good place to shop for local products such as pottery and the famous hand-woven palm-leaf baskets. You can also visit the mineral water springs at Siliyin, so take an empty bottle and fill up for free! Those with an interest in crafts will enjoy a visit to the weaving school at Fidimin where children learn to produce carpets, tapestries and embroideries. Lake Karun, to the northwest, is a pleasant spot to enjoy an alfresco lunch of freshly-cooked lake fish or to indulge in bird-spotting. Nearby fossil beds show the variety of animal life in the region millions of years ago. Inhabited since prehistoric times, Fayyum also has its share of antiquities, not least the ruined pyramids at Meidum, Lahun and Hawara. At Kom Ushim are the extensive remains of the ancient town of Karanis, including houses and a temple dedicated to the crocodile gods Pnepheros and Petesuchos. In ancient times this was a 'must' on every tourist itinerary, the chief attraction being the opportunity to feed titbits to the sacred crocodiles kept on the premises! There is also a small museum of local archaeology. To the northwest, at the far end of Lake Karun, are the remains of ancient Dionysias, with a Roman (see **A-Z**) fortress, public baths and temples.

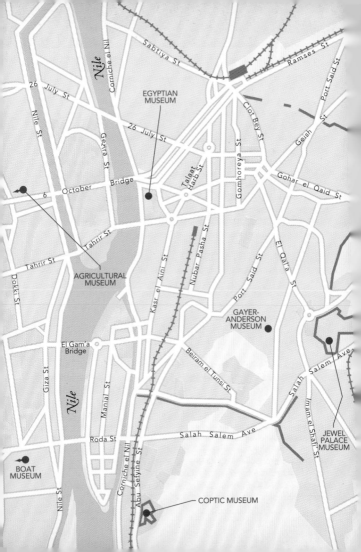

AGRICULTURAL MUSEUM Mathaf el Zirai St, Dokki.
❏ 0900-1400 Tue.-Sun.
The world's oldest agricultural museum, housed in large pavilions set in extensive gardens. Displays include ancient Egyptian farming techniques and tableaux of traditional rural life. Gardens suitable for picnics.

BOAT MUSEUM Giza, Pyramids. Next to the Great Pyramid.
❏ 0900-1600.
*Discovered in over a thousand pieces in a pit under the pyramid in 1954, the funerary boat of King Cheops (see **A-Z**) has been restored and is now displayed in a purpose-built museum. Almost 4500 years old, it is believed to be the oldest boat in the world. See **CAIRO-WALK 1**.*

COPTIC MUSEUM Mari Girgis, Old Cairo.
❏ 0900-1600 Sat.-Thu., 0900-1100, 1300-1500 Fri.
*Extensive and important collection of art and artefacts from the Christian period in Egypt, including icons, manuscripts and textiles. Gift shop, picnic facilities and café in gardens. See **CAIRO-WALK 2**, **A-Z**.*

EGYPTIAN MUSEUM Mariette Pasha St, Tahrir Sq., Central Cairo.
❏ 0900-1600 Sat.-Thu., 0900-1100, 1300-1600 Fri.
*World-famous museum of Egyptian antiquities from the Pharaonic and Graeco-Roman periods, including the treasures of Tutankhamun (see **A-Z**). Shops, cafeteria and gardens. See **A-Z**.*

GAYER-ANDERSON MUSEUM Bayt el Kritlya, Ahmed ibn Tulun Sq. Next to Ibn Tulun Mosque.
❏ 0800-1600 Sat.-Thu., 0800-1100, 1300-1600 Fri.
Two Ottoman-period houses restored by the British army officer and Orientalist Maj. Gayer-Anderson to serve as his home and private museum. A fascinating collection of mainly Islamic art.

JEWEL PALACE MUSEUM Citadel.
❏ 0900-1700.
*Small 19thC palace housing period furniture and costumes, and King Farouk's wedding throne. Cafeteria, picnic facilities. See **CAIRO-WALK 3**.*

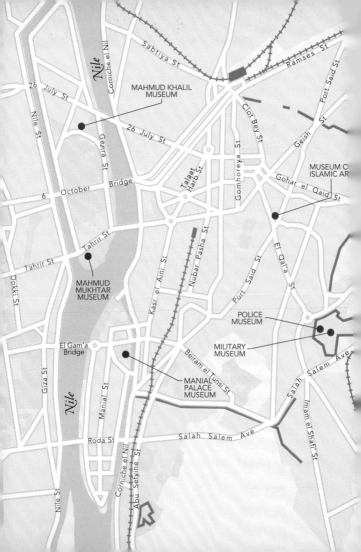

Nile

Sabtiya St

Corniche el Nil

Ramses St

Port Said St

26 July St

MAHMUD KHALIL
MUSEUM

Clot Bey St

Geish St

Nile St

26 July St

Gezira St

Talaat Harb St

Gomhoreya St

Gohar el Qaid St

MUSEUM O
ISLAMIC AR

6 October Bridge

Tahrir St

Tahrir St

Kasr el Aini St

Nubar Pasha St

Port Said St

El Qala St

Dokki St

Tahrir St

MAHMUD
MUKHTAR
MUSEUM

POLICE
MUSEUM

El Gam'a
Bridge

MILITARY
MUSEUM

Giza St

Manial St

MANIAL
PALACE
MUSEUM

Beram el Tunsi St

Salah Salem Ave

Nile

Roda St

Salah Salem Ave

Imam el Shafr St

Nile St

Corniche el Nil

Abu Setyine St

MAHMUD KHALIL MUSEUM 1 Sheikh el Marsafi St, Zamalek.
Behind the Marriott Hotel.
❑ 1000-1300, 1700-2000.
*Elegant Islamic building housing an interesting collection of objets d'art,
Impressionist paintings and sculptures. See* **CAIRO-ART GALLERIES**.

MAHMUD MUKHTAR MUSEUM Tahrir Gardens, Tahrir St,
Gezira. Next to Galaa Bridge.
❑ 0900-1500 Sat., Sun. & Tue.-Thu., 0900-1200 Fri.
*Delightful small museum designed by Ramses Wissa Wassef and dedi-
cated to the work of Egypt's great national sculptor. See* **Mukhtar**.

MANIAL PALACE MUSEUM 1 Manial Palace St, Roda Island.
❑ 0900-1600.
*Ex-royal palace dating from the beginning of the present century and
housing furnishings, family mementos and hunting trophies. The shady
gardens are a suitable place for picnics. See* **CAIRO-BUILDINGS &
MONUMENTS 3**, **A-Z**.

MILITARY MUSEUM Citadel.
❑ 0900-1700.
*Large exhibition covering Egyptian military history from Pharaonic times
to the present day. Displays include weapons and uniforms, plus paintings and models of important battles. See* **CAIRO-WALK 3**.

MUSEUM OF ISLAMIC ART Ahmed Maher Sq., Port Said St.
❑ 0900-1600 Sat.-Thu., 0900-1100, 1300-1600 Fri.
*Extensive collection of Islamic art, with an emphasis on the heritage of
Cairo. Shop and garden suitable for picnics. See* **A-Z**.

POLICE MUSEUM Citadel.
❑ 0900-1700.
*Housed in the Citadel's former prison, complete with dungeons, displays
cover the history of crime and punishment in Egypt from Pharaonic times
until today. There is also a fire-fighting display featuring veteran fire
engines. See* **CAIRO-WALK 3**.

Nile

Sabtiya St

Ramses St

YA SALAM

Port Said St

26 July St

Corniche el Nil

Nile St

Gezira St

EMPRESS NIGHTCLUB

26 July St

Clot Bey St

Geish St

FALAFEL

Talaat Harb St

Gomhoreya St

Gohar el Qaid St

6 October Bridge

BELVEDERE/ TROPICANA

Tahrir St

Tahrir St

El Qala St

Dokki St

Tahrir St

ALHAMBRA

EL SAMAR/ LAYALINA

Kasr el Aini St

Nubar Pasha St

Port Said St

El Gam'a Bridge

Giza St

Manial St

Beiram el Tunsi St

Salah Salem Ave

Nile

Salah Salem Ave

Imam el Shafi' St

Nile St

Roda St

Corniche el Nil

Abu Selyine St

ALHAMBRA Cairo Sheraton, Galaa Sq., Dokki, tel: 3488600.
❏ 2200-0300 Tue.-Sun. Reservations recommended. ❏ Admission inc.
dinner.
Said to have the best Middle Eastern floor show in Cairo. Formal dress.

BELVEDERE/TROPICANA Nile Hilton Hotel, Corniche el Nil,
Central Cairo, tel: 765666.
❏ 2130-0230 Wed.-Mon. Reservations recommended. ❏ Min. charge.
*Tropicana poolside club in summer, and Belvedere roof-top club for
winter (wonderful Nile views). International floor show plus belly
dancer. Formal dress in Belvedere.*

EL SAMAR/LAYALINA El Gezira Sheraton Hotel, Tahrir Gardens,
Gezira, tel: 3411555.
❏ 2200-0300. Reservations recommended.
*The place to catch performances by the top names in Middle Eastern
entertainment. Layalina is the open-air summer venue; El Samar is
indoors. Formal dress.*

EMPRESS NIGHTCLUB Cairo Marriott Hotel, Gezira Palace,
Zamalek, tel: 3408888.
❏ 2230-0300. Reservations recommended. ❏ Admission inc. dinner.
Oriental cabaret and dining. Formal dress.

FALAFEL Ramses Hilton Hotel, Corniche el Nil, Central Cairo,
tel: 758000.
❏ 1830-0100. Reservations recommended. ❏ Admission inc. dinner.
*Egyptian floor show with folk music and dance, comedy and belly
dancer – highly recommended. Early and late shows nightly. Formal
dress.*

YA SALAM El Salam Hotel, Abdel Hamid Badawi St, Heliopolis,
tel: 2455155.
❏ 2200-0300 Tue.-Sun. Reservations recommended. ❏ Min. charge.
*International floor show and belly dancer. À la carte dining. Formal
dress.*

Nile

Sabtiya St

Corniche el Nil

Ramses St

VITO'S/
SINDBAD

Port Said St

26 July St

Nile St

26 July St

Gezira St

Clot Bey St

Geish St

Gomhoreya St

JACKIE'S

6 October
Bridge

SULTANA

Talaat Harb St

Gohar el Qaid St

Tahrir St

Tahrir St

El Qala St

Tahrir St

LE
CAMELEON

Dokki St

REGINE'S

Kasr el Aini St

Nubar Pasha St

Port Said St

El Gam'a
Bridge

Giza St

Nile

Manial St

Abu Selyine St

Beiram el Tunsi St

Salah Salem Ave

Salah Salem Ave

Imam el Shafi' St

Roda St

Corniche el Nil

Nile St

NILE PHARAOH/
GOLDEN PHARAOH

JACKIE'S Nile Hilton Hotel, Corniche el Nil, Central Cairo.
❑ 2100-0230.
Cairo's longest established disco, back on the scene after a recent refurbishment. Teenagers' matinées Thu. and Fri. Hotel residents and members only.

LE CAMELEON Safir Hotel, Missaha Sq., Dokki.
❑ 2300-0300. ❑ Min. charge.
The current hot spot in all senses of the word! Also good for celebrity-spotting. Thu. night cabaret and monthly theme parties.

REGINE'S El Gezira Sheraton Hotel, Tahrir Gardens, Gezira.
❑ 2200-0300. ❑ Min. charge.
A sophisticated disco with panoramic views of the Nile. The supper menu includes steaks, grilled shrimp, etc. Hotel residents and members only.

SINDBAD Cairo Sonesta Hotel, Tayaran St, Heliopolis.
❑ 2130-0400. ❑ Min. charge.
Loud and popular disco with light show and all the latest hits.

SULTANA Semiramis Intercontinental Hotel, Corniche el Nil, Garden City.
❑ 2230-0330. ❑ Min. charge.
Plush new venue with high-tech lighting and video equipment. Regular theme nights and occasional teenagers' matinées.

VITO'S El Salam Hotel, Abdel Hamed Badawi St, Heliopolis.
❑ 1900-0300. ❑ Min. charge.
Dancing plus games corner including darts and backgammon. Supper menu featuring Italian specialities. Relaxed atmosphere.

NILE PHARAOH/GOLDEN PHARAOH Dock on Nile St, Giza.
Tel: 726713.
Dinner cruises with belly dancer aboard Pharaonic-style vessels. Also lunch cruises. See travel agents, or telephone for details.

Restaurants 1

GEZIRA GRILL Cairo Marriott Hotel, Gezira Palace, Zamalek, tel: 3408888.
❏ 1300-1600, 1900-2300. Reservation recommended. ❏ Expensive.
Housed in the former billiard rooms of the 19thC Gezira Palace (see CAIRO-BUILDINGS & MONUMENTS 3), the Gezira Grill is the very height of elegant dining in Cairo. French cuisine, rib roast and grills are all on the menu.

JUSTINE'S Four Corners, 4 Hassan Sabry St, Zamalek, tel: 3412961.
❏ 1230-1500, 1930-2300. Reservation recommended. ❏ Expensive.
Smart French restaurant offering inclusive business lunches as well as à la carte dining.

KHAN EL KHALILI 5 Badestan Lane, Khan el Khalili, tel: 903788.
❏ 1100-2330. ❏ Expensive.
This stylish new restaurant right in the heart of the bazaar area is one of the few to do justice to the subtlety of Middle Eastern cuisine. Ema soup is a delicately spiced combination of lamb and yoghurt. The mezze are also excellent (try sambousek, little pastry parcels with a savoury filling), as are the main courses and desserts. No alcohol.

LOLA 15 Rd 9B, Maadi, tel: 3515587.
❏ 1800-0100. Reservation recommended. ❏ Expensive.
Luxurious grill restaurant specializing in steaks and seafood. The Mama Lola Special is truly unforgettable.

MARCO POLO Meridien Hotel, Uruba St, Heliopolis, tel: 2905055.
❏ 1300-0100. Reservation recommended. ❏ Expensive.
This restaurant has fine Italian cuisine served to the accompaniment of live music.

THE MOGHUL ROOM Mena House Oberoi Hotel, Pyramids Rd, Pyramids, tel: 3877444.
❏ 1230-1430, 1930-2300. Reservation essential. ❏ Expensive.
The best Indian food in Cairo, served in the palatial setting of an ex-royal guesthouse, and accompanied by live Indian music.

Nile

Sabtiya St

Corniche el Nil

26 July St

Nile St

Gezira St

26 July St

LA CHESA

Ramses St

LE CHANTILLY

Port Said St

Clot Bey St

Geish St

Gohar el Qaid St

LA PIZZERIA

Talaat Harb St

Gomhoreya St

6 October Bridge

Tahrir St

Tahrir St

Tahrir St

Dokki St

LE CHALET/
LE CHÂTEAU

Kasr el Aini St

Nubar Pasha St

Port Said St

El Qal'a St

El Gam'a Bridge

Giza St

Manial St

Beiram el Tunsi St

Salah Salem Ave

Imam el Shafi' St

Nile

Roda St

Corniche el Nil

Salah Salem Ave

KHAN
EL KHALILI

Nile St

Abu Sefyine St

OMAM
RESTAURANTS

OMAM RESTAURANTS 6th Floor, Riyad Tower, Nile St, Giza, tel: 737592.
Reservations recommended. ❏ Expensive.
Café Cairo (Coffee shop) ❏ 1000-0100.
Chandani (Indian restaurant) ❏ 1930-0030.
El Fanous (Moroccan restaurant) ❏ 1300-1700, 1930-0030.
Il Camino (Italian restaurant) ❏ 1300-1700, 1930-0030.
Sakura (*Teppanyaki*-style Japanese restaurant) ❏ 1300-2400.
Five great restaurants. Elegant décor and some of the best food in Cairo. No alcohol.

SWISSAIR RESTAURANTS Le Chalet and Le Château, Nasr Building, 31 Nile St, Giza, tel: 3485321, La Chesa, 21 Adly St, Central Cairo, tel: 3939360 & Le Chantilly, 11 Baghdad St, Heliopolis, tel: 669026.
❏ Expensive.
Le Chalet ❏ 1000-2400.
Le Château ❏ 1300-1600, 2000-2400.
La Chesa ❏ 0800-2300 Sat.-Thu., 1200-2300 Fri.
Le Chantilly ❏ 0700-2330.
Continental cuisine with an emphasis on Swiss specialities. Le Chalet is a coffee shop offering daily specials; Le Château is more formal. La Chesa, Le Château and Le Chantilly all offer good-value lunches for businessmen.

KHAN EL KHALILI Mena House Oberoi Hotel, Pyramids Rd, Pyramids, tel: 3877444.
❏ 24 hr. ❏ Moderate.
Offers standard Continental menu; useful when visiting the Pyramids.

LA PIZZERIA Nile Hilton Hotel, Corniche el Nil, Central Cairo, tel: 765666.
❏ 1200-0200. ❏ Moderate.
Conveniently located for shopping or museum trips. Traditional pizzeria with open-air section for warm weather, and strolling musicians in the evening.

TIROL

Nile

Sabtiya St

Corniche el Nil

Ramses St

26 July St

ROY'S
RESTAURANT

Nile St

Gezira St

26 July St

Clot Bey St

Port Said St

Geish

STEAK
CORNER/
TANDOORI

6 October
Bridge

Talaat Harb St

Gomhoreya St

Gohar el Qaid St

ABU
ALY'S
CAFÉ

Tahrir St

Kasr el Aini St

Nubar Pasha St

El Qala St

Port Said St

Tahrir St

Dokki St

El Gam'a
Bridge

Giza St

Nile

Manial St

Beiram el Tunsi St

Salah

Imam el Shafi St

Salah Salem Ave

Roda St

Salah Salem Ave

Nile St

Corniche el Nil

Abu Setyine St

LOLITA'S

LOLITA'S 15 Rd 9B, Maadi, tel: 3515587.
❏ 1200-2400. ❏ Moderate.
Huge and imaginative Italian menu featuring some unusual pasta dishes. The restaurant has a cheerful, casual atmosphere, and there is also a weekly outdoor barbecue.

ROY'S RESTAURANT Cairo Marriott Hotel, Gezira Palace, Zamalek, tel: 3408888.
❏ 1200-2400. ❏ Moderate.
The big, juicy burgers are the best in Cairo! The regular Mexican buffet featuring chilli, tacos and all the trimmings is also highly recommended. Children's parties can be arranged.

STEAK CORNER 8 Amman Sq., Dokki, tel: 3497326.
❏ 1200-0100. ❏ Moderate.
For serious meat eaters, a comfortable restaurant specializing in steaks prepared in every imaginable way.

TANDOORI 11 Shehab St, Mohandiseen, tel: 3486301.
❏ 1200-2400. ❏ Moderate.
Excellent Indian food served in a cool, elegant environment. Delicious breads and tandoori dishes, plus a good range of vegetarian dishes – try the vegetable jalfarezi. No alcohol.

TIROL 38 Gezirat el Arab St, Mohandiseen, tel: 3449725.
❏ 1200-0100. ❏ Moderate.
Chalet-style restaurant serving Austrian specialities. Cheese fans will enjoy the rich cheese soup; the potato dumplings and veal dishes are also good.

ABU ALY'S CAFÉ Nile Hilton Hotel, Corniche el Nil, Central Cairo, tel: 765666.
❏ 1100-2300 summer, 1100-1700 winter. ❏ Inexpensive.
*Close to the Egyptian Museum (see **A-Z**), an open-air terrace café serving traditional Egyptian snacks like tamiyya or shawerma sandwiches with fresh juices, mint tea, etc.*

ABU SHAKRA 69 Kasr el Aini St, Central Cairo, tel: 848811, & New Club Rd, New Maadi, tel: 3521165.
❑ 1300-1700, 1900-2400. ❑ Inexpensive.
Popular kebab restaurants with authentic Cairo atmosphere. No alcohol.

AMIR FISH CENTER 90a Dawaran St, Shubra, tel: 642362.
❑ 0900-0400. ❑ Inexpensive.
Off the beaten track, but a 'must' for fish and seafood fans. Your choice from the huge displays is grilled or fried to order and served in the clean, simple restaurant. Exceptional value. No alcohol.

ANDREA 60 Mariotia Canal, Pyramids, tel: 3871133.
❑ 1300-1700, 1900-2300. ❑ Inexpensive.
Long-established open-air restaurant specializing in charcoal-grilled chicken and pigeon served with Egyptian salads.

EGYPTIAN PANCAKES 7 Khan el Khalili, tel: 90623.
❑ 1200-2400. ❑ Inexpensive.
Pavement café serving only fitir, the traditional Egyptian pancake, made to order with a variety of savoury or sweet fillings. No alcohol.

FELFELA 15 Hoda Sharaawi St, Central Cairo, tel: 3922751.
❑ 0700-0100. ❑ Inexpensive.
A favourite with local office workers, Felfela is packed at lunchtime but quieter in the evening. The extensive Egyptian menu includes a good selection of vegetarian dishes. Also does takeaways.

TIKEA 12 Khaled ibn el Walid St, Dokki, tel: 711470.
❑ 1200-0300 Thu.-Tue. ❑ Inexpensive.
Excellent Egyptian food; hungry people should try the fatta, a rich dish combining bread, meat and yoghurt with nuts and raisins. No alcohol.

TIKKA 47 Batal Ahmed Abdel Aziz St, Mohandiseen, tel: 3460393.
❑ 1000-2400. ❑ Inexpensive.
Indian snacks served with extraordinary giant puris. Good salad bar. No alcohol.

CENTRAL CAIRO
The city's main shopping area is focussed on Kasr el Nil and Talaat Harb Sts, with numerous department stores, fashion and shoe shops. This is the best place to look for dress fabrics, household linen and leather goods. The crowds can be horrific, though – nervous shoppers might prefer the comparative peace of the new shopping malls.

HELIOPOLIS
Every type of shopping from local bakers and greengrocers to fashion boutiques and department stores. The main area is Korba, stretching between Roxy Sq. and Baghdad St.

KHAN EL KHALILI BAZAAR
The original 'Old Bazaar in Cairo' is a confusing maze of narrow medieval streets lined with tiny shops and cafés. A shopper's dream, it is the place to buy handicrafts like brass and copper ware, glass and woodwork, jewellery and appliquéd textiles, as well as spices and per-fumes. Here, bargaining is definitely the order of the day. The bazaar is the quintessential Cairo experience – if you can't find something here, it probably doesn't exist! See A-Z.

MAADI
Centred around Rd 9, Golf and Old Maadi, Maadi's shopping districts feature small fashion boutiques, supermarkets, etc.

MOHANDISEEN
Definitely the place for fashion shopping with numerous boutiques, including well-known European chains like Benetton, Stefanel and NafNaf. Popular shopping streets include Batal Ahmed Abdel Aziz, Shehab and Gamaat el Dowal el Arabiyya.

ZAMALEK
Upmarket shopping with chic boutiques, art galleries and bookshops. A good place to find fashionable kids' and babies' wear. Most shops are concentrated along 26th July St and the streets running off it, notably Hassan Sabry and Shagarat el Durr.

Nile

Sabtiya St

Corniche el Nil

Ramses St

26 July St

Nile St.

CONCRETE/
MIX & MATCH

LEATHER HOME

Port Said St

Clot Bey St

Geish

26 July St.

Gezira St

THE SHIRT
SHOP

OCTOPUS

Gomhoreya St

Talaat Harb St

6 October Bridge

MM

Gohar el Qaid St

MOBACO

Tahrir St

Kasr el Aini St

Nubar Pasha St

Port Said St

El Qalra St

Dokki St

Tahrir St

MARIE
LOUIS/
BTM

Salah Salem Ave

Imam el Shafi St

El Gam'a Bridge

Giza St

Manial St

Beiram el Tunsi St

Nile

Roda St

Salah Salem Ave

Corniche el Nil

Nile St

Abu Seiyine St

CONCRETE 21 Mahad el Swisry St, Zamalek, 23 Ramses St, Korba, Heliopolis & 15 Rd 216, Maadi.
Men's fashion boutique – trousers, shirts, sweaters.

LEATHER HOME 3 Ishak Yaqub St, Zamalek & 107 Rd 9, Maadi. Also at the Cairo Sheraton & Semiramis Intercontinental hotels.
Good-quality leather shoes, bags and clothing.

MARIE LOUIS/BTM 1 Batal Ahmed Abdel Aziz St, Mohandiseen & Uruba St, Heliopolis.
Marie Louis stocks a good selection of quality women's business suits and separates. BTM has men's shirts, jackets and trousers.

MIX & MATCH 21 Mahad el Swisry St, Zamalek & 23 Ramses St, Korba, Heliopolis.
Ladies' fashion boutique – suits, dresses and separates.

MM 28 Talaat Harb St, 8 Kasr el Nil St & the Nile Hilton, all in Central Cairo. Also at 110 26th July St, Zamalek, Ard el Golf, Maadi & Uruba St, Heliopolis.
Popular chain of shoe shops also selling bags, belts and leather jackets.

MOBACO 19 Talaat Harb St, 242 Sudan St, Mohandiseen, & the Nile Hilton & Semiramis Intercontinental hotels, all in Central Cairo. Also at 47 Beirut St, Heliopolis & 31 El Mukhtar St, Maadi.
Egyptian chain selling stylish quality cotton casual wear for men and women: shirts, slacks, skirts and jackets.

OCTOPUS 8 Marsafi Sq., Zamalek, 6 Arhab St, Giza, 25 Misr Helwan Agricultural Rd, Maadi (near the Maadi Hotel), 15 Baghdad St & 92 Hegaz St, Heliopolis.
Colourful cotton casuals, including sweatshirts, tracksuits and T-shirts.

THE SHIRT SHOP Shopping Galleria, Cairo Marriott Hotel, Gezira Palace, Zamalek.
Men's business and casual shirts, all in fine Egyptian cotton.

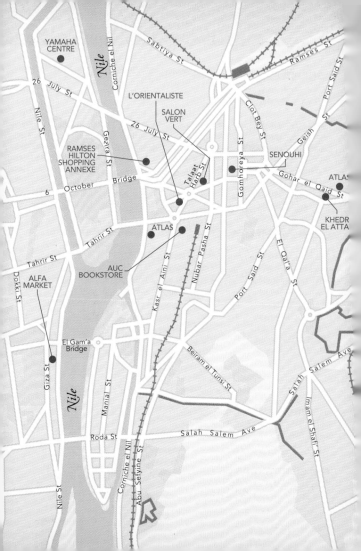

Shopping 3

ALFA MARKET 1st floor, Riyad Tower, Nile St, Giza.
Western-style supermarket good for stocking up on drinks and snacks. Gifts, toys and sportswear section upstairs.

ATLAS Badestan Lane, Khan el Khalili & Semiramis Intercontinental Hotel, Corniche el Nil, Garden City.
Fine textiles include Egyptian silk and hand-woven cotton from Akhmim. Garments made to order.

AUC BOOKSTORE American University in Cairo, 113 Kasr el Aini St, Central Cairo. Entrance on Mohammed Mahmud St.
❑ Closed Fri.
Best English-language bookshop in Egypt. Guides and maps, plus fiction, non-fiction and reference. Good for background reading on Egypt.

KHEDR EL ATTAR Muizz li Din St, Khan el Khalili.
Incredible old shop selling spices and herbal remedies.

L'ORIENTALISTE 15 Kasr el Nil St, Central Cairo.
A Cairo institution, specializing in old Orientalist books and prints.

RAMSES HILTON SHOPPING ANNEXE Behind the Ramses Hilton Hotel, Corniche el Nil, Central Cairo.
Cool, quiet shopping mall with outlets for clothes, shoes, gifts, etc., plus a café and Japanese restaurant.

SALON VERT Kasr el Nil St, Central Cairo.
Three stores specializing in fabrics and household linen – sheets and tablecloths, dress fabrics, upholstery material, etc.

SENOUHI 5th floor, 54 Abdel Khalek Sarwat St, Central Cairo.
*Authentic ethnic jewellery and textiles, prints and drawings, Wissa Wassef (see **A-Z**) tapestries and batiks.*

YAMAHA CENTRE Taha Hussein St, Zamalek.
Smart new mall with shops for fashions, home furnishings, etc.

Sports & Activities

CAIRO HASH HOUSE HARRIERS
❏ Weekends, tel: 3475633.
*Welcome runners of all standards to their weekly fun runs, which are followed by various social activities. A great way to meet people. Events are announced in the press (see **Newspapers**), or telephone for details.*

CAIRO STADIUM Heliopolis.
❏ Matches 1500 Fri. & Sat. (Sep.-May).
Soccer is Egypt's national sport, and attracts a huge following. Cairo Stadium is home to the two biggest Cairo teams, Ahly and Zamalek.

GEZIRA RACETRACK Zamalek, next to Gezira Sporting Club.
❏ Alternate weekends Oct.-May.
*Horse racing on grass. The racecard is published in the Sat. Egyptian Mail (see **Newspapers**).*

GEZIRA SPORTING CLUB Gezira Palace St, Zamalek.
Comprehensive sports facilities include golf, tennis, squash, horse riding, swimming and bowls. Temporary membership available.

SAKKARA PALM CLUB Sakkara Tourist Rd, Sakkara.
Swimming, horse riding, squash and tennis; landscaped gardens make this the place to escape the bustle of Cairo. Day membership available.

SALEM BALLOONS Tel: 2991946 or book through travel agents.
*Spectacular flights over Cairo and the Pyramids (see **A-Z**) followed by a sumptuous buffet breakfast in the desert. See **Ballooning**.*

SPLASH HEALTH CLUB Cairo Marriott Hotel, Gezira Palace, Zamalek.
Gymnasium with sauna, Jacuzzi and Turkish baths, plus swimming, tennis and aerobics. Temporary membership available.

THE SHOOTING CLUB Nady el Seyd St, Dokki.
Organizes game shooting and fishing on a regular basis; can advise on regulations, protected species, etc. Temporary membership available.

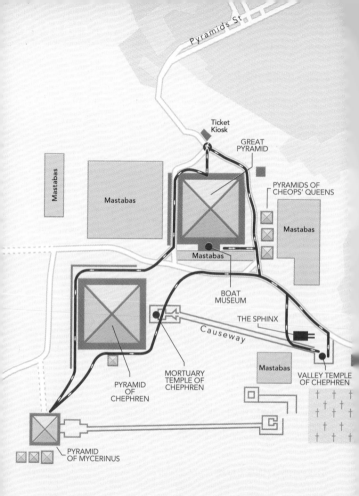

Pyramids St

Ticket
Kiosk

GREAT
PYRAMID

PYRAMIDS OF
CHEOPS' QUEENS

Mastabas

Mastabas

Mastabas

Mastabas

Mastabas

BOAT
MUSEUM

THE SPHINX

Causeway

MORTUARY
TEMPLE OF
CHEPHREN

Mastabas

VALLEY TEMPLE
OF CHEPHREN

PYRAMID
OF
CHEPHREN

PYRAMID
OF MYCERINUS

Walk 1

*By bus or taxi for a walk round the Pyramids (see **A-Z**). Duration: 2 hr 45 min.*

Begin at the ticket kiosk near the entrance to the site; if you wish to enter any of the monuments you will need to buy the relevant tickets here. If arriving by taxi, arrange for the driver to wait for you here. The Pyramids of Egypt are the only one of the Seven Wonders of the World to have survived intact. Ahead is the most famous, the Great Pyramid (see **A-Z**), constructed for the pharaoh Cheops (see **A-Z**) around 2500 BC. The entrance used by visitors is said to have been cut in the 9thC on the orders of the caliph Ma'mun who believed treasure was hidden inside; the original entrance can be seen above it.
Continue around the base of the pyramid, noticing, as you turn the corner, the cemetery on the right. The mastabas (see **A-Z**) here belonged to those courtiers and royal relatives granted the privilege of burial near their divine masters. Notice also, on the left, the smooth limestone blocks around the base of the pyramid. All pyramids were originally cased in polished stone, most of which was pillaged in later times. Immediately ahead, however, the Pyramid of Chephren retains enough of its casing to give an impression of its original appearance.
Continue around Chephren's pyramid to the third, much smaller, Pyramid of Mycerinus. This was never completed, as can be seen from the unpolished stones left in its granite casing. Behind are three small pyramids which belonged to royal women.
Return to Chephren's pyramid, passing another subsidiary pyramid, before arriving at the ruins of the Mortuary Temple, where offerings were once made to the dead king's spirit. It was connected to the Valley Temple by a covered causeway, part of which survives. Around the Mortuary Temple were pits to contain boat burials.
Returning to the road, continue downhill towards the Sphinx (see **A-Z**). Carved from the living rock, it represents Chephren as the defender of Egypt. The best view is from the causeway, accessible from the Valley Temple. The temple itself is impressive, faced inside and out with finely worked red granite. Numerous sculptures, including the famous statue of Chephren in the Egyptian Museum (see **A-Z**), were found here.
Follow the path through the temple and along the causeway beside the

Sphinx, turning right to return to the road. Ahead and to the left, next to the Great Pyramid, is a modern building housing Cheops' reconstructed funerary boat. When turning the corner to visit the Boat Museum (see **CAIRO-MUSEUMS 1**), notice the fine porticoed Tomb of Seshemnefer. On leaving, turn left, following the road past the small pyramids of Cheops' queens to return to the car park.

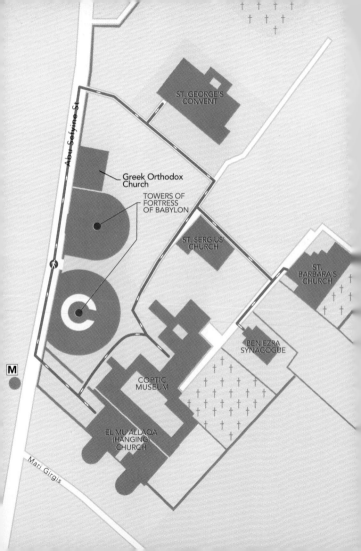

ST. GEORGE'S
CONVENT

Greek Orthodox
Church

TOWERS OF
FORTRESS
OF BABYLON

ST. SERGIUS
CHURCH

ST.
BARBARA'S
CHURCH

BEN EZRA
SYNAGOGUE

COPTIC
MUSEUM

EL MU'ALLAQA
(HANGING)
CHURCH

Abu Sefyne St

Mari Girgis

M

Walk 2

By taxi, water bus or Metro to Mari Girgis for a walk round Old Cairo (see A-Z). Duration: 2 hr.

Start at the gate of the Coptic Museum. The round towers facing you are part of the Fortress of Babylon (see A-Z), the oldest extant building on this site. Instead of entering the museum turn left and walk past the Greek Orthodox Church to where a flight of steps (signposted to the churches of St. Barbara and St. Sergius) descends from the modern to the ancient street level. Follow the path, a typical example of a medieval street, a short distance to a door in the wall on the left. This is the entrance to St. George's Convent, worth visiting for its grand hall, once part of a Fatimid (see A-Z) palace.

Coming out, turn left and continue along the path. At the corner, turn right, following the sign to St. Barbara's Church and ignoring the arch on the left. Notice the interesting old doors in the walls here. Take the next left – St. Barbara's (see A-Z) is facing the end on the left. There was a church on this site from very early times, but most of the present building dates to the 11thC; the fine sanctuary screen, of wood inlaid with ivory, is from the 13thC. Coming out, turn left and walk the few steps to the Ben Ezra Synagogue (see A-Z) next door. This building dates from the 12thC and despite its plain exterior has some fine decorative work inside. It is currently under restoration, but remains open to the public.

Leaving Ben Ezra, turn right and retrace your steps, turning left just before St. Barbara's. At the corner, turn left under a low arch; the entrance to St. Sergius' Church (see A-Z) is on your left. One of Cairo's earliest churches, the oldest part of the building dates from the 8thC and was constructed over the cave where the Holy Family is said to have stayed during the Flight into Egypt. On leaving, turn left and follow the path up two short flights of steps into the Coptic Museum Gardens. The ticket office and gift shop are on your right, the museum to the left.

A 'must' on every visitor's itinerary, the Coptic Museum (see A-Z) houses extensive and well-displayed collections of architectural stone and woodwork, manuscripts, textiles, glass and pottery. Coming out of the museum, turn left, past the WCs and cafeteria, and pass through the

Coptic Museum

archway to visit El Mu'allaqa church, which was constructed over part of the Fortress of Babylon – hence its name, which translates as the Hanging Church (see **A-Z**). Dating mainly from the 11thC, it has been renovated many times; it is best known for its very fine inlaid wood-work. Coming out, walk straight ahead to leave by the entrance porch. Turn right onto the street, and after a few steps you are back at the Coptic Museum gate.

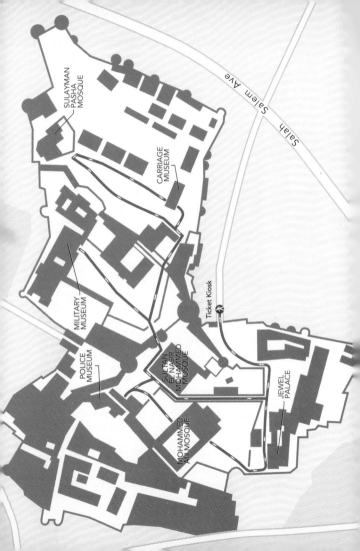

Salah Salem Ave

SULAYMAN PASHA MOSQUE

CARRIAGE MUSEUM

MILITARY MUSEUM

POLICE MUSEUM

SULTAN EL NASIR MOHAMMED MOSQUE

MOHAMMED ALI MOSQUE

Ticket Kiosk

JEWEL PALACE

Walk 3

By taxi for a walk round the Citadel (see **A-Z***). Duration: 2 hr 30 min.*

Begin at the main car park; facing the gate, the walls on the right are part of Saladin's original fortifications, while those on the left date from the 19thC. The ticket kiosk is just inside the entrance; after paying for admission, follow the path uphill (via the steps to the cafeteria) to the Jewel Palace (see **CAIRO-MUSEUMS 1**). For over 700 years, Egyptian rulers lived in the Citadel; this palace was begun in 1814 by Mohammed Ali (see **A-Z**). It now houses displays of furnishings once the property of the ex-royal family, including King Farouk's (see **A-Z**) wedding chair. On coming out, pause on the terrace to enjoy the magnificent panoramic view of Cairo – on a clear day, you can see the Pyramids (see **A-Z**). Anyone who has been to Istanbul will recognize the Ottoman style of the Mohammed Ali Mosque (see **A-Z**) with its twin pencil minarets. Begun in 1824, it is also known as the Alabaster Mosque because of the lavish use of that stone. On leaving, walk downhill to the Police Museum (see **CAIRO-MUSEUMS 2**), located in the Citadel's former prison and housing displays on crime and punishment from Pharaonic times to the present day. Across the courtyard is the mosque of Sultan el Nasir Mohammed, dating from the 14thC; notice the unusual minarets with their ceramic decoration and the reused classical columns in the colonnade.

Leaving the mosque, walk round to the right and go through the gateway, keeping to the right and following the signs to the Sulayman Pasha Mosque. Set in a shady garden, this charming little mosque, begun in 1528, was the first Ottoman mosque in Egypt. It is a peaceful spot, seldom visited, and the guardian will be happy to show you around. Retracing your steps toward the gate, you may wish to stop at the Carriage Museum, housing vehicles once used by the royal family. Instead of turning left to the gate, follow the path ahead and to the right to visit the Military Museum (see **CAIRO-MUSEUMS 2**). Located in the Harem Palace, once the family residence of Mohammed Ali, it is worth a visit for the splendid apartments alone. Its displays cover Egyptian military history from the Pharaonic period to modern times. A cafeteria and WCs are located in the south wing. On leaving, follow the path through the gateway and back to the main entrance.

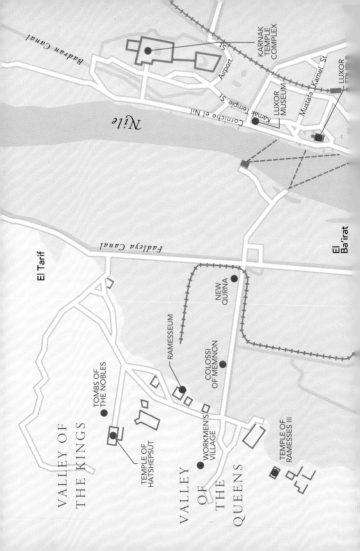

Buildings & Monuments 1

WEST BANK

West Bank monuments are generally open 0600-1800 summer, 0600-1600 winter, but may be closed without notice. Tickets must be purchased in advance from the kiosk at the tourist ferry landing. Half-price student tickets are available on production of a card from the Egyptian Antiquities Organization office near the Colossi of Memnon. Cross from the East Bank by either the tourist or the local ferries. Taxis can be hired near the tourist and local ferry landings; donkeys are available at the local ferry landing only. Bicycles can be taken on the local ferry.

VALLEY OF THE KINGS
*Tombs of the New Kingdom pharaohs, painted with brightly-coloured mythological scenes. See **A-Z**.*

VALLEY OF THE QUEENS
*Tombs of the New Kingdom queens and princes. See **A-Z**.*

WORKMEN'S VILLAGE Deir el Medina.
*Village and necropolis of the royal tomb builders; it contains some of the most beautiful and best-preserved private tombs. See **A-Z**.*

COLOSSI OF MEMNON
*Two colossal seated statues of Amenhotep III (see **A-Z**) which once fronted his now-vanished mortuary temple. See **A-Z**.*

TEMPLE OF RAMESSES III Medinet Habu.
*The sprawling remains of Ramesses III's (see **A-Z**) complex, including temples, chapels, houses and palaces. See **A-Z**.*

TEMPLE OF HATSHEPSUT Deir el Bahari.
*The elegant mortuary temple of the famous female pharaoh. See **A-Z**.*

TOMBS OF THE NOBLES Sheikh Abd el Qurna.
*Tombs of high officials of the New Kingdom, renowned for their vivid paintings of ancient daily life. See **A-Z**.*

Karnak

Buildings & Monuments 2

RAMESSEUM
*The romantic ruins of the mortuary temple of Ramesses II (see **A-Z**), containing the fallen colossus which inspired Shelley's poem Ozymandias. See **A-Z**.*

NEW QURNA
*Built by Hassan Fathy (see **A-Z**) in the 1940s, New Qurna was intended as a prototype for model villages throughout Egypt, but it did not prove popular with the local inhabitants and is now largely abandoned.*

EAST BANK

KARNAK TEMPLE COMPLEX Karnak.
❏ 0600-1800 summer, 0600-1700 winter.
Huge, impressive temple complex built over a period of 2000 years. See **LUXOR-WALK 2, A-Z**.

LUXOR MUSEUM Corniche el Nil.
❏ 1700-2200 summer, 1600-2100 winter, 0800-1200 Ramadan.
*Modern, well laid out museum displaying finds from the Luxor area, including some objects from the tomb of Tutankhamun (see **A-Z**). See* **LUXOR-WALK 1, A-Z**.

LUXOR TEMPLE Corniche el Nil.
❏ 0600-2200 summer, 0600-2100 winter.
A beautiful small temple located in the town centre. See **LUXOR-WALK 1, A-Z**.

DENDERA

BIRTH HOUSE

Coptic Church

Roman Bath

TEMPLE OF HATHOR

Sacred Lake

Qena

Qus

Luxor

DENDERA

Nile

WESTERN DESERT

ABYDOS

ABYDOS

TEMPLE OF RAMESSES II

TEMPLE OF SETI I

OSIREION

Excursion 1

By road to Abydos and Dendera. Organized excursions are available.

For visitors based in Luxor, the trip to Abydos and Dendera is an excellent opportunity to see something of agricultural life in the Egyptian countryside. During the sugar cane harvest every spring and autumn, endless convoys of laden donkeys and camels plod along the road; at other seasons you may see farmers ploughing or threshing, or irrigating their fields with the traditional shaduf. In use since Pharaonic times, this ingenious device lifts water by means of a leather bucket suspended on a pole. It requires a great deal of effort to operate and is rapidly being replaced by the diesel pump.

Abydos (see **A-Z**), approximately 160 km northwest of Luxor by road, was the cult centre of the god Osiris, Lord of the Underworld. From the earliest times, Egyptians of all walks of life aspired to be buried there; many of those unable to do so erected cenotaphs instead.

The Temple of Seti I (see **A-Z**) is famous for its delicate raised limestone reliefs, considered by many to be the finest in Egypt. Begun by Seti himself and completed by his son Ramesses II (see **A-Z**), its unusual design incorporates seven chapels dedicated to the principal gods of Egypt. Behind is a curious underground structure known as the Osireion and possibly connected with the rites of rebirth. From here a path across the desert leads to the ruined Temple of Ramesses II.

The route from Abydos to Dendera is particularly scenic, passing through picturesque mudbrick villages clustered along the canal banks. Dendera (see **A-Z**), approximately 90 km east of Abydos, was the cult centre of the goddess Hathor, patroness of love, beauty and music. An ancient site, the present temple dates from the Graeco-Roman period. Its capitals are adorned with images of the goddess as a beautiful woman with cows' ears. The Birth House, to the right of the entrance, has some fine reliefs of the emperor Trajan. Inside the temple itself, you can explore the crypts before climbing the stairs to the roof for a marvellous view over the temple precincts.

On the return journey, why not stop at the craftsmen's village of Garagos (see **A-Z**), 30 km north of Luxor, where it is possible to take a close look at village life. You can also visit the pottery and weaving workshops.

Nile

CORNICHE

HIGH DAM/
TEMPLE OF ISIS/
TEMPLES OF KALABSHA & BEIT EL WALI

OBELISK

OLD CATARACT
HOTEL

MUSEUM

NILOMETER

ELEPHANTINE
ISLAND

KITCHENER
ISLAND

BOTANICAL
GARDENS

TOMBS

MONASTERY
OF ST. SIMEON

MAUSOLEUM
OF THE
AGA KHAN

Excursion 2

By road, rail or air 220 km south to Aswan. Organized excursions are also available.

Aswan (see **A-Z**) is situated on the First Cataract of the Nile, a granite outcrop which in ancient times marked the boundary between Egypt and Nubia. Its location on the main African caravan routes made it until modern times an important market for such exotic goods as gold and ivory. Even today a visit to the bazaar, with its wealth of sights, sounds and smells, is an experience not to be missed.

The modern town retains a strongly African flavour, due in part to its largely Nubian population. Sauntering along the Corniche, watching the countless white-sailed feluccas (see **A-Z**) against the backdrop of the desert, one has a curious sensation of being beside the sea.

Formerly a small town, the High Dam project (see **A-Z**), completed in 1970, brought a huge influx of workers and engineers, many of whom chose to remain.

Besides the High Dam itself, there is much to interest the visitor to Aswan. The beautiful Graeco-Roman Temple of Isis at Philae, known in classical times as the 'Pearl of the Nile', was submerged for almost 80 years before a rescue operation relocated it on Agilka Island. Other rescued monuments include the Nubian temples of Kalabsha and Beit el Wali, which together with a pretty kiosk from Kertassi have been reconstructed at an attractive site beside Lake Nasser.

On the outskirts of the town lie the ancient granite quarries, where an enormous obelisk lies partially cut from the bedrock. A pleasant felucca ride will take you to Elephantine Island with its ancient Nilometer (see **A-Z**) and museum of local antiquities, or to Kitchener Island, home of the lovely Botanical Gardens. On the Nile's west bank lie the rock-cut tombs of Old and Middle Kingdom officials with their impressive causeways. A more modern mausoleum nearby is the resting place of the Aga Khan (see **A-Z**); from here you can take a camel ride to visit the ruined 6thC Monastery of St. Simeon (see **Monasteries**).

For romantics, there is only one way to end a visit to Aswan: sipping tea on the terrace of the Old Cataract, an elegant turn-of-the-century hotel once frequented by Agatha Christie and featured in the film of her book *Death on the Nile*.

AL SUKKAREYA BAR Luxor Sheraton Hotel, El Awameya,
tel: 384544.
❏ 0800-0100.
Popular meeting place, with live entertainment in the evening.

CASINO Hilton International Luxor, New Karnak, tel: 384933.
❏ 2000-0400.
Slot machines, roulette, blackjack. Play in foreign currency. Foreigners only; bring passport identification.

FELLAH'S TENT Movenpick Jolie Ville Hotel, Crocodile Island,
tel: 384855.
❏ 1630-2100 (twice a week).
Oriental Night includes a sunset felucca cruise, oriental dinner and entertainment including folkloric music, snake show, belly dancer and horse show.

HARLEQUIN DISCO Hilton International Luxor, New Karnak,
tel: 384933.
❏ 2100-0400.
Bar and music for dancing.

LE LOTUS Novotel, Khaled ibn el Walid St, tel: 384887.
❏ 2230-late. ❏ Min. charge.
Shipboard bar and disco. Smart dress required; admission at management's discretion.

M/S MERI RA Luxor Sheraton Hotel, El Awameya, tel: 384544.
❏ 1900-2230 (three times a week).
Dinner cruises with bar and five-course gourmet dinner.

SABIL DISCO PLM Etap Hotel, Corniche el Nil, tel: 580944.
❏ 2230-0200. ❏ Min. charge.
Luxor's most popular disco; attracts mainly package tourists. There is a DJ and occasional theme evenings. Couples only; smart dress is required.

Nile

Airport St

Corniche el Nil

Temple St

Karnak

Badran Canal

FLAMBOYANT/
LE CHAMPOLLION

Ahmos St

Mustafa   Kamel   St

Station St

Salakhana St

BADOUR
FLOATING
RESTAURANT

Lokanda St

Mohammed

Corniche el Nil

Ahmad

Farid St

Orabi St

JOLIE VILLE
RESTAURANT

MOVENPICK
RESTAURANT

WHITE
CORNER

CLASS
RESTAURANT

LE BELVEDERE

FLAMBOYANT PLM Etap Hotel, Corniche el Nil, tel: 580944.
❏ 1930-2230. ❏ Expensive.
French cuisine in an elegant setting.

JOLIE VILLE RESTAURANT Movenpick Jolie Ville Hotel,
Crocodile Island, tel: 384855.
❏ 1230-1530, 1830-2300. ❏ Expensive.
Renowned lunch and dinner buffets – don't miss the chocolate mousse!

MOVENPICK RESTAURANT Movenpick Jolie Ville Hotel,
Crocodile Island, tel: 384855.
❏ 1230-1530, 1830-2400. ❏ Expensive.
À la carte restaurant serving snacks at lunchtime and sophisticated
European cuisine in the evening. Children's menu.

WHITE CORNER Isis Hotel, Khaled ibn el Walid St, tel: 383366.
❏ 1130-1500, 1830-2300. ❏ Expensive.
Seafood speciality restaurant.

BADOUR FLOATING RESTAURANT Corniche el Nil. Opposite
the Old Winter Palace Hotel. Tel: 383458.
❏ 1200-2400. ❏ Moderate.
Vast Egyptian/Lebanese menu. For something different try laban omo –
lamb cooked in yoghurt – or *shourbet badour, a peanut and garlic soup.*

LE BELVEDERE Novotel, Khaled ibn el Walid St, tel: 384887.
❏ 0530-2400. ❏ Moderate.
Breakfast, lunch and dinner buffets, plus Nile-side barbecue.

LE CHAMPOLLION PLM Etap Hotel, Corniche el Nil, tel: 580944.
❏ 24 hr. ❏ Moderate.
Coffee shop serving snacks and light meals. Daily pasta buffet.

CLASS RESTAURANT Khaled ibn el Walid St, tel: 386327.
❏ 1000-0100. ❏ Moderate.
Smart new restaurant offering Egyptian and international menus.

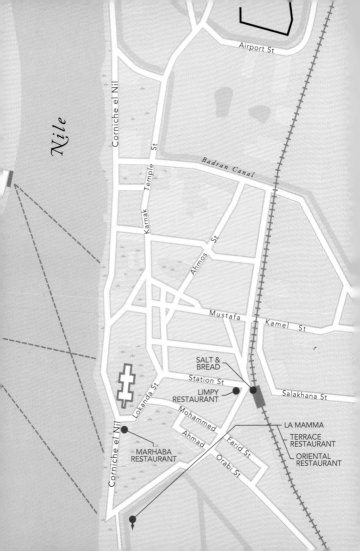

LA MAMMA Luxor Sheraton Hotel, El Awameya, tel: 384544.
❏ 1200-2400. ❏ Moderate.
Open-air Italian restaurant by a picturesque garden pool; an accordionist entertains in the evenings. Excellent pizzas, pastas and grills.

TERRACE RESTAURANT Luxor Sheraton Hotel, El Awameya, tel: 384544.
❏ 1200-1600. ❏ Moderate.
Open-air charcoal grill specializing in burgers, chicken and steak – all served with delicious baladi *bread brought hot to the table.*

LIMPY RESTAURANT Station Sq., tel: 382041.
❏ 0700-0100. ❏ Inexpensive.
Small, clean and air conditioned with a cheerful ambience, Limpy is popular with students. Egyptian/international menu – steaks, kebabs, omelettes and possibly the best chips in Egypt! No alcohol.

MARHABA RESTAURANT Tourist Bazaar, Corniche el Nil, tel: 382633.
❏ 1000-2300. ❏ Inexpensive.
This pleasant open-air terrace overlooking the Nile attracts budget travellers. Egyptian menu – try shakshouka *or grilled pigeon followed by* om ali. *No alcohol.*

ORIENTAL RESTAURANT Khaled ibn el Walid St. Opposite the Isis Hotel. Tel: 348093.
❏ 0700-0100. ❏ Inexpensive.
Clean and simple, a haunt of budget travellers. Small but good Egyptian/international menu. Try the meat paper – lamb and vegetables cooked in a parcel. Breakfasts and packed lunches can also be provided. No alcohol.

SALT & BREAD Station Sq. No telephone.
❏ 0800-2300. ❏ Inexpensive.
Unpretentious student restaurant offering some egg and vegetarian dishes. Try their massive Egyptian breakfast. No alcohol.

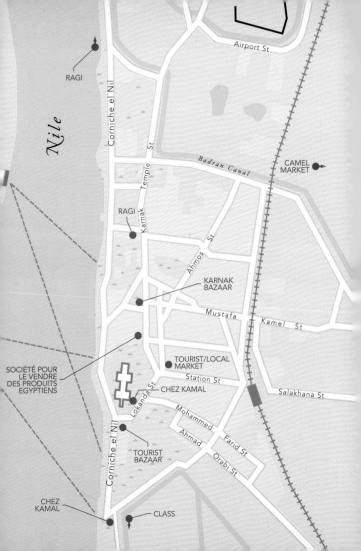

Nile

RAGI

Airport St

Corniche el Nil

Temple St

Badran Canal

CAMEL MARKET

RAGI

Karnak St

Amos St

KARNAK BAZAAR

Mustafa Kamel St

SOCIÉTÉ POUR LE VENDRE DES PRODUITS EGYPTIENS

TOURIST/LOCAL MARKET

Station St

CHEZ KAMAL

Lokanda St

Mohammed Farid St

Ahmad St

Orabi St

Salakhana St

Corniche el Nil

TOURIST BAZAAR

CHEZ KAMAL

CLASS

CAMEL MARKET El Hibel Village, 4 km east of Luxor.
❏ Tue. am.
Go early to catch the action!

CHEZ KAMAL Novotel & opposite the Luxor Hotel.
❏ 0800-2230.
Shirts and galabeyas ready to wear and made to measure. Also tailoring and copying of garments. 3-hr service.

CLASS Khaled ibn el Walid St. Near the Isis Hotel.
Fashionable cotton clothing, leather bags and jackets, shoes, jewellery and souvenirs. Expensive, but good quality.

KARNAK BAZAAR Karnak Temple St.
Papyrus paintings, and cheap and cheerful bead jewellery.

RAGI Nefertiti St (Dr Labib Habachi St) & opposite the Hilton International Luxor, New Karnak.
Gold and silver jewellery; specializes in Pharaonic designs set with semi-precious stones. Pieces made to order.

SOCIÉTÉ POUR LE VENDRE DES PRODUITS EGYPTIENS Karnak Temple St.
Three-floor government department store. Apart from textiles, the merchandise is uninspiring, but it's worth a visit to get an idea of local prices.

TOURIST BAZAAR Corniche el Nil.
Small shopping centre for books and cards, galabeyas, photographic materials, etc.

TOURIST/LOCAL MARKET Suq St.
❏ Daily.
The end of the road nearest the town centre has all kinds of souvenirs – rugs, brass, leather, etc. Further down, there are stalls for fruit and vegetables, spices and household goods. See LUXOR-WALK 1.

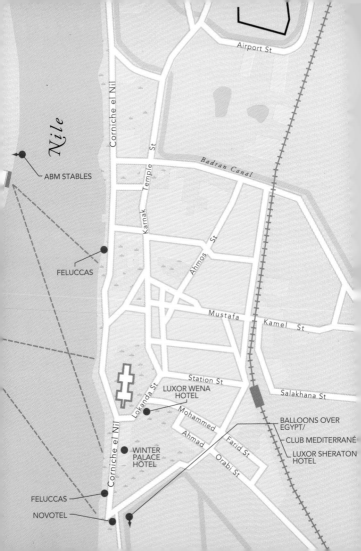

Nile

ABM STABLES

Corniche el Nil

Temple St

Badran Canal

Karnak

Airport St

Ahmos St

FELUCCAS

Mustafa   Kamel   St

Station St

Salakhana St

Lokanda St

LUXOR WENA
HOTEL

Mohammed

Ahmad

Farid St

BALLOONS OVER
EGYPT/

CLUB MEDITERRANÉ

LUXOR SHERATON
HOTEL

Orabi St

Corniche el Nil

WINTER
PALACE
HOTEL

FELUCCAS

NOVOTEL

Sports & Activities

ABM STABLES West Bank. Near the local ferry landing.
Stables offering organized rides and horses for hire; some hotels will make the arrangements for you. Donkeys can be hired in the same area.

BALLOONS OVER EGYPT El Rawda el Sharifa St, tel: 386515, or book at desks in major hotels.
❑ Oct.-May (twice daily, weather conditions permitting).
The experience of a lifetime! See **Ballooning**.

CLUB MEDITERRANÉE Khaled ibn el Walid St.
❑ 0800-1800.
Swimming pool available to non-residents. Day membership required.

FELUCCAS
Feluccas (see **A-Z***) can be hired from moorings along the Corniche; check the official tariff before agreeing a fee.*

LUXOR SHERATON HOTEL El Awameya, tel: 384544.
❑ Pool 0900-1700, tennis courts 24 hr.
Swimming pool and floodlit tennis courts open to non-residents on payment of a charge. Equipment is included in court hire, and a coach is available at extra charge. Table tennis, volleyball and croquet are also available, and fishing tackle can be hired. Contact Guest Relations.

LUXOR WENA HOTEL Town centre. Behind Luxor Temple.
❑ 0800-2000.
Swimming pool available to non-residents for a small charge.

NOVOTEL Khaled ibn el Walid St.
❑ 0900-1700.
Large floating pool open to non-residents for a daily charge. Also table tennis and volleyball.

WINTER PALACE HOTEL Corniche el Nil.
Floodlit tennis court available for hire by non-residents. Extra charge for equipment hire.

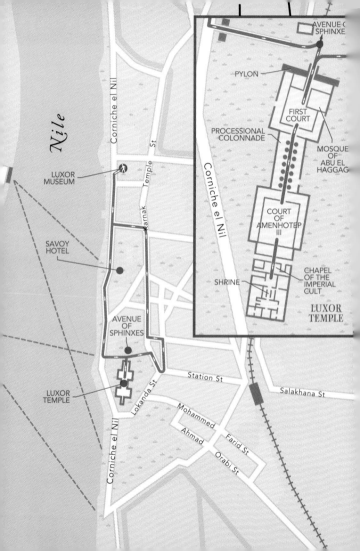

Nile

Corniche el Nil

Temple St

Karnak St

LUXOR MUSEUM

SAVOY HOTEL

AVENUE OF SPHINXES

LUXOR TEMPLE

Corniche el Nil

Lokanda St

Station St

Mohammed Farid St

Ahmad Orabi St

Salakhana St

Corniche el Nil

AVENUE OF SPHINXES

PYLON

FIRST COURT

PROCESSIONAL COLONNADE

MOSQUE OF ABU EL HAGGAG

COURT OF AMENHOTEP III

CHAPEL OF THE IMPERIAL CULT

SHRINE

LUXOR TEMPLE

Walk 1

A walk round the city centre, temple and museum areas of Luxor.
Duration: 2 hr.

Start at Luxor Museum (see **A-Z**), a stylish modern building housing a
well-displayed collection of antiquities from the Luxor area. After visiting, walk south along the Corniche; with its trees and views of the Nile
(see **A-Z**) it is the perfect spot from which to watch the sunset, perhaps
from the terrace of the old Savoy Hotel. Continue to the entrance to
Luxor Temple (see **A-Z**).

After paying for admission, follow the path, turning left and walking a
short distance along the avenue of sphinxes to get a good view of the
pylon. Built by Ramesses II (see **A-Z**) in the 13thC BC, it depicts scenes
of his famous battle against the Hittites at Kadesh. In front of it is a single obelisk; its twin now graces the Place de la Concorde in Paris.

Walk back along the avenue, which connects this temple with Karnak
(see **A-Z**), and enter the first court. Largely the work of Ramesses II, it is
surrounded by colossal statues of him. In one corner is the medieval
mosque of a local saint, Abu el Haggag; its height indicates the depth
to which the temple was once buried.

Passing between the twin seated colossi of Ramesses II, enter the processional colonnade. The walls to either side showing scenes of festival
processions probably date from the reign of Tutankhamun (see **A-Z**).
Continuing, walk through the colonnaded court of Amenhotep III (see
A-Z) to a small room adapted by the Romans into a chapel of the
Imperial cult; painted figures of emperors can be seen in the niche.
Through the door in the niche are the inner chambers of the temple,
including a shrine built by Alexander the Great (see **A-Z**) for the sacred
boat of the god Amun, to whom the temple was dedicated.

Retrace your steps to the pylon and leave by the exit on the right which
leads into the public park. Cross Karnak Temple Street to the road junction and turn left down Suq Street (Abdel Hamid Taha Seoudi Street),
passing the colourful displays of rugs and brassware, spices and vegetables (see **LUXOR-SHOPPING**). At Cleopatra Street turn left and then right
into Karnak Temple Street with its rows of small tourist shops. Continue
to Nefertiti Street (Dr Labib Habachi Street) and turn left to return to the
Corniche; turn right along the Corniche to go back to the museum.

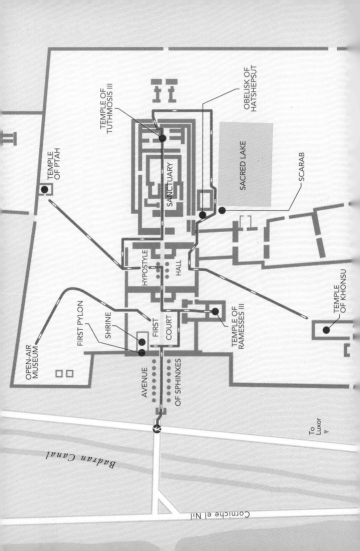

OPEN-AIR MUSEUM

TEMPLE OF PTAH

TEMPLE OF TUTHMOSIS III

OBELISK OF HATSHEPSUT

SANCTUARY

SACRED LAKE

SCARAB

HYPOSTYLE HALL

FIRST PYLON

SHRINE

FIRST COURT

TEMPLE OF RAMESSES III

TEMPLE OF KHONSU

AVENUE

OF SPHINXES

Badran Canal

Corniche el Nil

To Luxor

Walk 2

A walk round Karnak. Duration: 2 hr.

Begin at the main entrance to Karnak
(see **A-Z**). After paying for admission at
the ticket kiosk, cross the small wooden
bridge to a stone platform with two
small obelisks. This is the quay, used in
ancient times for waterborne processions. From here there is a fine view
along the main axis of the complex
which is approached by an avenue of
ram-headed sphinxes.

Walk between them and through the unfinished first pylon to pass into
the first court. Inside the entrance on the left is a triple shrine built by
Seti II for the sacred boats of Amun, Mut and Khonsu, to whom the
temple was dedicated. Just beyond is the entrance to the open-air
museum.

In the centre of the court are the remains of a huge kiosk built by the
Nubian pharaoh Tarhaqa, while on the right is a small temple of
Ramesses III (see **A-Z**): two statues of the king guard the entrance. After
exploring the temple, return to the main axis, passing a colossal stand-
ing statue of Ramesses II (see **A-Z**) to enter the hypostyle hall.

Perhaps the finest achievement of ancient Egyptian architecture, this
hall was begun by Seti I (see **A-Z**) and completed by Ramesses II; it is
interesting to compare Seti's delicate raised reliefs on the left-hand side
with his son's cruder, sunk reliefs on the right. Turning left, leave the
hall by the transverse aisle and turn right to admire the battle scenes of
Seti I on the outside wall; from here a path runs to the Temple of Ptah.
Continue along the wall, turning right and then left to rejoin the main
axis. The obelisk of Tuthmosis I is on the right and that of his daughter
Hatshepsut (see **A-Z**) on the left. Continue towards the sanctuary, noticing in front of it the two beautiful columns representing the lotus and
papyrus, symbols of Upper and Lower Egypt (see **A-Z**). The inside of
the sanctuary is covered with reliefs of offering scenes, and the pedestal
for Amun's sacred boat is still in place.

Turning right, walk around the outside of the sanctuary and across the gravel court, site of the oldest part of the temple. Beyond is the memorial temple of Tuthmosis III (see **A-Z**) with its unusual columned hall. During the Christian era it was used as a church, and traces of paintings of saints can still be seen. An interesting room at the back is often referred to as the botanical garden or the zoo because of its reliefs recording the exotic flora and fauna discovered during the king's campaigns.

Follow the path, crossing over a wooden walkway to the area behind the temple, and turn right towards the Sacred Lake, which was used for purification rites and perhaps the enactment of sacred dramas. There is a cafeteria on the right. Continue ahead, passing a huge stone scarab and turning right past the tip of a fallen obelisk belonging to Hatshepsut.

The door in the far corner opens onto the temple's transverse axis, a series of pylons arranged at right angles to the main axis; these are currently under restoration. Re-enter the hypostyle hall by the door ahead, taking time to admire the reliefs of Ramesses II. A path running from the door on the left leads to the Temple of Khonsu. From here you can retrace your steps to the main entrance.

Abydos: Approximately 160 km north of Luxor, Abydos was the necropolis of the ancient city of This, and the cult centre of the god Osiris. The Temple of Seti I is justly famous for its delicate limestone reliefs and well-preserved colours. Begun by Seti I (see **A-Z**) himself and completed by his successor Ramesses II (see **A-Z**), the temple's unusual design incorporates seven chapels dedicated to the principal gods of Egypt. Other monuments in the area include the Temple of Ramesses II. See **LUXOR-EXCURSION 1**.

Abu Simbel: Situated on the shores of Lake Nasser, close to the Sudanese border, the famous temples of Abu Simbel date to the reign of Ramesses II (see **A-Z**). Between 1966 and 1972 a massive rescue operation took place to raise them to safety above the water level. There are two temples at the site: the Great Temple, dedicated to Ramesses and some of the chief gods of Egypt, and the Small Temple, built for Queen Nefertari (see **A-Z**) and dedicated to the goddess Hathor.

Accidents & Breakdowns: Egyptians are very friendly people, always prepared to offer help in an emergency. If you are involved in a street accident, the police will soon arrive at the scene to render assistance: tourist police usually speak some English. See **Driving, Emergency Numbers**.

Accommodation: Both Cairo and Luxor offer a wide range of accommodation from youth hostels and camp sites to five-star luxury hotels, some housed in former royal palaces. Prices vary accordingly. Tourist information offices will assist individuals in finding accommodation, but groups must use a travel agent. It is worth investigating the flight and hotel packages offered by major tour operators, as these can work out both cheaper and far less trouble than making your own arrangements. See **Camping & Caravanning, Tourist Information, Youth Hostels**.

Admission Charges: The whole system of admission fees to museums and monuments is currently under review; it is therefore not possible to give guidelines at present. Students get a 50% reduction on

admission fees on production of an International Student Card.
Ticket/s: tazkara/tazaakir; How much?: bi kam?

Aga Khan Mausoleum: Located on the west bank of the Nile at
Aswan, this Fatimid-style granite and marble mausoleum was constructed in 1957 to serve as the resting place of the late aga, Sir Sultan
Mohammed Shah, leader of the Ismaili Muslims and grandfather of the
present Aga Khan. See **LUXOR-EXCURSION 2**.

Airports: Located in the northwestern suburb of Heliopolis, Cairo
International Airport, tel: 2914255, is about 45 min by bus or taxi from
the city centre. There are three passenger terminals: Terminal One for
Egyptair domestic and international flights, Terminal Two for international flights only, and Terminal Three for flights operated by Saudia,
which are mainly pilgrim flights to Mecca. Luxor International Airport,
tel: 384655, is located 12 km from the city centre; buses and taxis are
available. Both airports have cafeteria facilities, and duty-free shopping
is available on both arrival and departure.
Internal flights operate between major cities and resorts including
Cairo, Alexandria, Luxor, Aswan, Abu Simbel and Hurghada. The
major operator is the national airline Egyptair, which has offices in
some of the larger Cairo hotels and at 9 Talaat Harb St in Central Cairo,
tel: 3922835. The Luxor branch is at the Old Winter Palace Building,
Corniche el Nil, tel: 580581.
Entry and exit formalities can be lengthy, so allow plenty of time when
checking in for an international flight. All baggage, not just hand lug-
gage, is X-rayed whether travelling on internal or international flights.
Civilian airports double as military air bases, so photography is forbidden – keep cameras in bags to prevent misunderstandings.

Akhenaten (c.1350-1334 BC): Hailed by many as the first
monotheist, the pharaoh Akhenaten is one of the most striking and
memorable figures in Egyptian history. In an attempt to limit the over-
weening power of the priesthood of Amun, he tried to introduce a new
cult focussed on a formerly obscure deity – the Aten, or sun-disc.
Abandoning Thebes (see **A-Z**), he moved with his wife Nefertiti and

their daughters to a new capital near present-day Tell el Amarna. The so-called Amarna Period is characterized by a distinctive style of art, easily recognized by its naturalism and fluidity. It was, however, short-lived, as Akhenaten's reforms did not gain popular support and the measures he introduced to enforce them only hastened the inevitable backlash which followed his death. Within a short time the capital was returned to Thebes, and the cult of Amun reinstated under his young son, Tutankhamun (see **A-Z**).

Alcohol: Although Egypt does produce wines and beers for home consumption, Islamic strictures against the drinking of alcohol are widely observed, and drunken behaviour in public is unthinkable. Restaurants outside the major hotels and tourist establishments do not always serve alcohol, and on certain religious feasts it cannot be sold at all. Duty-free alcohol can be purchased on entry and at the duty-free shops in Cairo. See **Drinks**.

Alexander the Great (356-323 BC): When Alexander the Great invaded Egypt in 332 BC, he was welcomed as its deliverer from Persian oppression. A Macedonian by birth, Alexander was a great Egyptophile, and wasted no time in having himself declared the son of Amun and invested as pharaoh. His reign, however, was brief, as he died while on campaign in Persia in 323 BC; his body was returned to the new capital, Alexandria (see **A-Z**). Following Alexander's death, the government of Egypt passed into the hands of his general Ptolemy Soter, who founded his own dynasty, the Ptolemies (see **A-Z**).

Alexandria: El Iskanderiyya. Alexander the Great (see **A-Z**) planned the city which bears his name to serve as the capital of his empire. But he was never to see it completed, since he died on campaign in Persia in 323 BC – just nine years after his conquest of Egypt. His body was returned to Alexandria for burial, but the site of his tomb, the Soma, is lost. However, as the capital of Egypt under the Ptolemies (see **A-Z**) and the Romans (see **A-Z**), Alexandria grew and prospered, establishing a reputation as a centre of learning and commerce throughout the civilized world.

It was also one of the first centres of Christianity (see **A-Z**): during the Byzantine (see **A-Z**) period, it was the focus of many important theological disputes. With the fragmentation of the Byzantine Empire, the city went into a long period of decline until it was revived as a port and commercial centre by Mohammed Ali (see **A-Z**). Although somewhat eclipsed in this role by the Suez Canal ports, Alexandria today is Egypt's second city: with a population of three million it serves as a business centre, port and summer resort for the masses of Cairo. See **CAIRO-EXCURSION 2**.

Alphabet & Numerals: Most visitors find themselves thoroughly confused by Arabic writing – not surprisingly, for in addition to the multiplicity of scripts in use, each character has four different forms! Fortunately, most public notices, street names and shop signs are also written in English. The numerals, however, are quite easy to learn: a useful tip is to study car numberplates which usually have the number written in both Arabic and Western-type figures. Knowing your numerals really pays off when shopping, as often prices are written in Arabic only.
Numbers: 1: wahed; 2: itnein; 3: talaata; 4: arba'a; 5: khamsa; 6: sitta; 7: sab'a; 8: tamaniya; 9: tis'a; 10: 'ashara; 11: hedashar; 12: itnashar; 13: talaatashar; 14: arba'tashar; 15: khamastashar; 16: sittashar; 17: saba'tashar; 18: tamantashar; 19: tisa'tashar. 20: ishrin; 30: talatin; 40: arba'in; 50: khamsin, etc. 100: miyya; 1000: alf. 21: wahed w'ishrin; 22: itneen w'ishrin, etc. 101: miyya wa wahed; 102: miyya w'itneen, etc. 1001: alf wa wahed; 1002: alf w'itneen, etc. The first: el awwal; the second: et taani; the third: et talaat, etc.

Amenhotep III (c.1386-1349 BC): Amenhotep III was one of Egypt's best-loved pharaohs, the father of the heretic king Akhenaten (see **A-Z**) and the grandfather of Tutankhamun (see **A-Z**). His reign produced some fine works of art, and his monuments include Luxor Temple (see **A-Z**) and the Colossi of Memnon (see **A-Z**).

Antiquities & Antiques: Ever since an antiquities market has existed, dealers in forged Egyptian artefacts have reaped large sums

Alexandria

from gullible buyers. Some of these fakes are good enough to fool even the experts, as many well-known museums have found to their embarrassment. Genuine Pharaonic antiquities are available, but only through licensed dealers, who are controlled by the Antiquities Department. In order to export such items, a special permission must be granted by the department, and this is virtually impossible to obtain. The same rule applies to any object over 100 years old, including Islamic and European antiques.

Aqueduct: Over 3 km long, the Aqueduct dates from the Mamluk (see **A-Z**) period, though it was in use until the late 19thC. Linking the Citadel (see **A-Z**) with the Nile, its massive tower housed the huge wooden water wheels which raised the water from the river. See **CAIRO-BUILDINGS & MONUMENTS 2**.

Architecture: Few countries can offer such a wealth of architectural styles as Egypt, from the monumentality of the Pharaonic era to the pioneering work of modern architects such as Hassan Fathy (see **A-Z**). However, while its ancient monuments are world-famous, the heritage of the past 2000 years goes largely ignored. This is a bonus for the

enterprising traveller, who can escape the crowds at the Pyramids to explore the delights of Cairo's mosques, churches, palaces and cara-vanserais in perfect peace. Cairo is also a veritable directory of modern architectural styles, from rococo to post-modernist. No lover of Art Nouveau or Art Deco should leave without taking a walk around some of the residential districts such as Garden City, or enjoying a contemplative coffee in one of the period cafés.

Art Galleries: The best time to explore Cairo's thriving modern art scene is during the exhibition season which runs Oct.-May. Exhibitions last about two weeks and are held in both private and public galleries; most work is for sale. Galleries normally close during the middle of the day but stay open late in the evening; check local press for details of exhibitions, venues and times. See **CAIRO-ART GALLERIES**.

Aswan: Located 220 km south of Luxor, and sited on the First Cataract of the Nile, Aswan is both an expanding industrial town and a popular tourist centre. Places to visit include the High Dam (see **A-Z**), the Temple of Isis at Philae, the granite quarries and the Botanical Gardens. See **LUXOR-EXCURSION 2**.

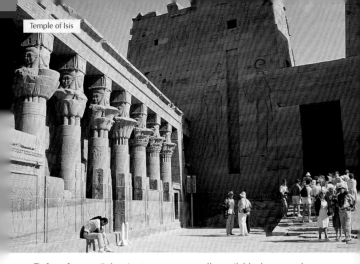
Temple of Isis

Baby-sitters: Baby-sitters are not generally available, but some larger hotels may be able to arrange this service. See **Children**.

Baksheesh: Rooted in the Islamic practice of almsgiving, the original concept of baksheesh was a form of giving which conferred blessings on both donor and recipient. Today the term covers both tipping in general and the now widespread practice of cadging from tourists, which has become a real nuisance. Small children, for example, will frequently demand baksheesh in the form of sweets and pens: it is highly inadvisable to comply, as the result is often fighting among the children and increasingly aggressive behaviour towards tourists. In some areas tourist police have to be deployed to keep the children at bay; the authorities would like to see the practice eliminated, but this depends on visitors' cooperation. A donation to a suitable charity is a more appropriate and practical way to help these children and their families. See **Charities**.

Ballooning: For the ultimate memory of Egypt, a hot-air balloon flight over the Giza pyramids or the monuments of Luxor is a 'must'. Weather conditions permitting, flights take place twice a day, at dawn

and in the afternoon during the winter season, and include sumptuous buffet breakfasts or teas while the balloon is inflated and packed. Flights last between 45 min and 2 hr, depending on the wind. Views are spectacular, and the gentle speed of the balloon is perfect for aerial photography. See **CAIRO-SPORTS & ACTIVITIES, LUXOR-SPORTS & ACTIVITIES**.

Banks: See **Currency, Money, Opening Times**.

Bargaining: Bargaining for what you buy is a way of life in Egypt, and visitors either love or hate it; those who hate it are probably better off sticking to fixed-price stores. When bargaining, decide in advance the maximum you are prepared to pay, and don't allow pushy salesmen to bully you. A really good bargaining session may involve walking off and being dragged back several times before a price is settled, so allow plenty of time and get into the spirit of the game – some great bargains await the persistent!

Can I buy . . .?: mumkin ishtiri . . .; Can I see . . .?: mumkin ashuf . . .; this . . .: da . . .; How much?: bi kam; Very expensive!: ghali awi!; No, thank you: la', shukran; OK: mashi.

Bayt el Suhaymi: An excellent example of a wealthy home of the Ottoman (see **A-Z** period). The leafy courtyard and ground floor, including a magnificent reception room with an inlaid marble fountain, were the male domain. The women's quarters, upstairs, were also sumptuously decorated and fitted with latticework windows which allowed the occupants to look out without being seen. Here also were private quarters, a bathroom and a loggia where the owner could sit to enjoy the cool evening breeze. See **CAIRO-BUILDINGS & MONUMENTS 2**.

Beaches: Egypt's most popular beach resorts are located either on the Red Sea (Hurghada, Sharm el Sheikh) or along the Mediterranean coast (Alexandria, Mersa Matruh). From Cairo there are regular buses to all resorts plus flights to Sharm el Sheikh and Hurghada. Hurghada is only a 4-hr drive from Luxor; there are three buses a day and twice-weekly flights. Resorts offer a wide range of accommodation, from simple beach camps to luxury hotels, and a variety of water sports including scuba diving and snorkelling along the Red Sea reefs.

Ben Ezra Synagogue: Dating from the 12thC, this is claimed to be Egypt's earliest synagogue. Its plain exterior belies the elaborate decoration inside; note the carved marble pulpit and fine woodwork inlaid with mother of pearl and ivory. See **CAIRO-BUILDINGS & MONUMENTS 1, WALK 2.**

Best Buys: Egypt offers a wealth of bargains to the discerning shopper able to resist the barrage of trashy overpriced souvenirs. Top value at about a quarter of European prices is casual fashion wear made locally in pure Egyptian cotton. Quality shirts are also an excellent buy, either off the peg or made to measure; a local tailor will often make an original or copy a favourite garment in a matter of hours. Choose your fabric from the wide range of cottons and silks available from department stores or specialist shops. For something more exotic, try a

galabeya, the traditional Egyptian robe; in cotton it makes a practical housecoat or poolside cover-up, in richly embroidered silk it becomes a stunning evening gown. Other textile bargains include household linen and furnishing fabrics and beautiful hand-embroidered or appliquéd cushion covers, bedspreads and wall hangings. Local workshops also produce rugs and carpets – best buys are the flat-woven wool rugs with lively geometric designs or village scenes.

Leather clothing, shoes and accessories can also be good value, but pay close attention to quality, as this can be extremely variable. Gold and silver jewellery and precious and semi-precious stones are popular souvenirs, but it is essential to be well-informed before parting with your money, as many tourists have found to their cost. Shop only at reputable dealers, and *never* make a purchase without shopping around first. Both gold and silver should be hallmarked – most gold is 18 carat, and silver pieces should be stamped with the silver content of the metal – 600, 800 or 900. Jewellery is sold by weight, with a small percentage added for workmanship; check the daily gold price, published in the *Egyptian Gazette*, before buying. Great caution should be exercised when buying stones, as glass and plastic imitations abound – unless you really know what you are doing, your money is probably best spent elsewhere.

Traditional craft products make beautiful and practical souvenirs – choose from copper or brass lamps, trays and tables, intricately carved and inlaid wooden boxes, screens and furniture, carved alabaster or light, colourful Muski glassware. Whatever you select will be a unique reminder of Egypt. See **CAIRO-CRAFTS**, **SHOPPING 1-3**, **LUXOR-SHOPPING**, **Bargaining**, **Papyrus**, **Shopping**.

Bicycle & Motorcycle Hire: Cycling is not recommended in Cairo, but it is a very popular way to explore the monuments and countryside around Luxor, and there are many rental places. Some of the largest are located near the station, behind Luxor Temple and opposite the Emilio Hotel in Yussef Hassan St. If you bargain well, the price is very reasonable. Some hotels also rent bicycles, but these are much more expensive. Bicycles are not available on the West Bank, but they can be taken over on the local ferry.

Bird-watching: Egypt is an ornithologist's dream, especially during the spring and autumn migrations when vast flocks of storks, pelicans and smaller birds pass through on their journey between Africa and Europe. The wide range of habitats, from deserts to marshes and coastal areas also ensures a rich variety of resident species from the ubiquitous egrets and kingfishers to the rare Egyptian vulture. A useful small guide, *Common Birds of Egypt*, is published by the American University in Cairo (see **CAIRO-SHOPPING 3**).

Boats: In Cairo, river buses run from the terminus at Maspero (north of the Ramses Hilton, opposite the Radio and Television building). Routes go north to the Nile Barrages and south to Old Cairo, calling at Dokki, Manial, Roda and Giza en route. In Luxor, there are two ferry services to the West Bank – the tourist ferry which has landings in front of the PLM Etap and Winter Palace hotels, and the local ferry, which has landings in front of Luxor Temple and beside the Novotel. The Movenpick Jolie Ville Hotel also has a courtesy boat running between Crocodile Island and Luxor Temple.

Bookshops: Most large hotels have a bookshop (*maktaba*) stocking a range of English-language books and magazines. For a wider selection, try the following – Cairo: AUC Bookstore (see **CAIRO-SHOPPING 3**), Al Ahram (Nile Hilton and branches); Luxor: Aboudi (Tourist Bazaar), A. A. Gaddis (Old Winter Palace Building).

Botanical Gardens: Egypt's warm climate and fertile soil make it a gardener's paradise. The Orman Botanical Gardens, located on Giza St in Dokki (next to Cairo Zoo), are open 0800-1700 in summer and

0800-1600 in winter. Laid out during the last century, they contain a variety of labelled specimens. The gardens of the Agricultural Museum (see **CAIRO-MUSEUMS 1**) also house many interesting trees, plants and shrubs. The Botanical Gardens on Aswan's Kitchener Island are well worth a visit for the variety of exotica (see **LUXOR-EXCURSION 2**).

Buses: Cairo's public buses are overcrowded and unpleasant, but from 10 PT a ride, unbeatable value. They can be recognized by their blue and white or red and white livery; the route numbers are written in Arabic. The main terminus is at Tahrir Sq. – some useful routes from there include 8 to the Pyramids, 174 to the Citadel and 400 to the airport. There is also a minibus service from Tahrir; minibuses are more comfortable and more expensive at 25-50 PT a ride. Useful routes: 27 to the airport, 82 to the Pyramids. Long-distance air-conditioned buses also run between Cairo and major cities. Buses for Alexandria depart from Tahrir Sq., for destinations in Upper Egypt including Luxor and Hurghada from Ahmed Helmi Sq., north of Ramses station. Remember that many of the large hotels operate courtesy buses to popular central destinations such as the Egyptian Museum and Khan el Khalili. Luxor's local buses – covered pick-up trucks – can be hard to identify at first, but it is worth the effort as they are by far the cheapest way to get about the locality, with fares from around 15 PT. Don't forget to stamp your feet to let the driver know where you want to be dropped! As with Cairo, comfortable long-distance buses connect Luxor with other cities, and there is a frequent service to Hurghada on the Red Sea. The terminus for both local and long-distance buses is behind Luxor Temple, opposite the Horus Hotel. Again, many of the larger hotels offer a regular free shuttle bus service to the town centre; check in reception for the timetable.

Byzantines: When the emperor Constantine (AD 323-37) moved his capital from Rome to Constantinople, Egypt became a province of the Byzantine Empire. During this time Christianity (see **A-Z**) was first tolerated and later adopted as the official religion. In 641, the Byzantine forces were routed by the Arabs and Egypt became a part of the Arab Empire.

Cafés: From medieval times coffee houses have been the focus of Cairene social life, and in their role as meeting places they have influenced the course of modern Egyptian history. Although still chiefly a male preserve, there are many cafés which women visitors can use, and no visit is complete without sampling their unique atmosphere. See **CAIRO-CAFÉS**.

Cairo Tower: Borg el Qahira. A relic of the Nasser (see **A-Z**) era, the distinctive lotus silhouette of the Cairo Tower is a familiar feature of the Cairo skyline. Rising to a height of 187 m, on a clear day the tower affords fine views over the city from its restaurant, cafeteria and viewing platform. See **CAIRO-BUILDINGS & MONUMENTS 3**.

Calèches: Calèches, known to the locals as *hantours*, are the picturesque horse carriages found everywhere in Luxor and increasingly in Cairo too. They provide a pleasant and relaxing way of sightseeing, especially during warm weather. Calèches can be found outside major hotels or they can be hailed in the street. In Luxor, the official fare tariff is displayed at calèche stands, in the tourist information office and in hotels; check it in advance, as there are some unscrupulous drivers.

Cameras & Photography: Egypt is a photographer's paradise, but be prepared for both very bright light and heavy shadow; some photographers recommend a polarizing filter. Photography is permitted in some museums on purchase of a ticket, but flash is not normally allowed. The same is true of tombs, where you must purchase a ticket for each tomb you wish to photograph. Photography at most open-air sites is free. Video cameras are subject to a different set of rules and must be declared at customs on arrival in Egypt. Permits for video cameras tend to be expensive, and their use is forbidden at some sites. The numerous camera shops in both Cairo and Luxor can undertake simple repairs, and film, batteries, etc. are cheap and widely available. Always ask before photographing someone, as they may object – if they agree, you will usually be expected to pay them. Be very careful not to photograph any subject – airports, bridges, etc. – which could be construed as military, and do not attempt to photograph people in uniform.

Camping & Caravanning: Camping facilities are very limited in Egypt. However, camp sites close to Cairo abound in the Pyramids area. There is a camp site in Luxor at the YMCA Camp, Karnak Temple St, tel: 382425.

Car Hire: Few visitors to Egypt rent self-drive cars, as it is far simpler and often cheaper to hire a taxi or limousine by the day or week. If you do want to rent a car, you must be over 25 and in possession of an International Driving Licence; you will also need to produce your passport and a large deposit or credit card. Major rental companies have desks in all the large Cairo hotels. There are no facilities for car rental in Luxor. See **Driving**, **Taxis**.

Charities: Many visitors to Egypt are moved by the plight of some of its less fortunate inhabitants, but are at a loss as to how to help. The following Cairo-based organizations all welcome donations: CARE International Egypt, 18 Hoda Sharaawi St, Apartment 1, PO Box 2019, Central Cairo, tel: 3935262 (rural development projects); Catholic Relief Services, 13 Ibrahim Naguib St, Garden City, tel: 3558034 (industrial and agricultural development); El Nur wal Amal, 16 Abu

Bakr el Sedik St, Heliopolis, tel: 22437772 (voluntary-run school for blind girls); Brooke Animal Hospital, 2 Bairam el Tonsi St, Sayeda Zeinab, tel: 849312 (helps sick and injured animals and their owners – visitors are welcome here or at their Luxor branch, located behind Luxor Temple). Also in Luxor, the voluntary-run hospital at Garagos is always in need of money – donations can be left at the Catholic church on Karnak Temple St.

Chemists: Chemists (*agzakhana* or *farmaseyya*) are found all over Cairo and in the centre of Luxor (there are several along Station St). They can often be identified by signs bearing a cup and serpent or a crescent, and frequently stay open late at night. Many pharmacists speak English and can advise on common ailments. See **Health**.

Cheops (c.2589-2566 BC): The builder of the Great Pyramid (see **A-Z**): Cheops is the Greek version of the Egyptian name Khufu.

Children: Apart from the dangers of traffic, Egypt is completely safe for children, who will be universally fussed over, indulged and, if lost, promptly returned. There are lots of fun activities and excursions for children of all ages, and plenty of pocket money-priced shopping – carved wooden dolls, printed T-shirts, crocheted Nubian hats and mini-*galabeyas* – which also make suitable gifts to take home for children. See **CAIRO-CHILDREN**, **Baby-sitters**.

Christianity: According to tradition, Christianity was brought to Egypt by the apostle Mark in the 1stC, but it was not until the 4thC that it was established as the state religion under the emperor Theodosius. Today, about 10% of Egypt's population is Christian, the vast majority of these belonging to the Coptic Orthodox Church. Copts are Monophysites, believing in the single nature of Christ as God and man. They have their own pope, and enjoy a strong sense of their own identity and tradition.

Churches: There are many interesting examples of churches to be visited in Egypt, particularly in the area of Old Cairo (see **A-Z**). The entrance to a Coptic church is via the narthex, a transverse hall. This leads into the body of the church, which has a central nave and two side aisles. This is separated from the sanctuary area by a screen, often richly decorated, displaying icons of Christ, the Virgin and saints. Visitors are always made welcome at services – remember that men and women always sit on separate sides of the church and that it is customary for women to cover their hair.

Cinema: There are dozens of cinemas in Cairo; those listed below all show mainly English-language films. In addition, some large hotels have outdoor film shows during the summer; check the local press for details. The Cairo Film Festival (see **Events**) is a great opportunity to see the latest films from around the world.
Cairo Sheraton Cinema, Cairo Sheraton Hotel, Giza St, Dokki, tel: 3488600; El Salam Cinema Centre, El Salam Hotel, Abdel Hamid Badawi St, Heliopolis, tel: 2455155; Metro, 35 Talaat Harb St, Central Cairo, tel: 757566; Tahrir, Tahrir St, tel: 714726. See **Newspapers**, **What's On**.

Citadel: Qalaa. Begun by Saladin (see **A-Z**) in the 12thC and enlarged by succeeding generations, the Citadel was home to all the rulers of Egypt up to 1874. The Citadel commands magnificent views across the city and its massive walls enclose a fascinating collection of monuments, including mosques, palaces and museums. See **CAIRO-BUILDINGS & MONUMENTS 2**, **MUSEUMS 1 & 2**, **WALK 3**.

City of the Dead

City of the Dead: Cairo's great medieval cemeteries lie to the east of the city. The two main areas are known as the Northern and Southern cemeteries; both contain many fine mausoleums. The most famous, the complex of Qaitbey (see **A-Z**), is located in the former. See **CAIRO-BUILDINGS & MONUMENTS 2**.

City Walls: The Khan el Khalili Bazaar (see **A-Z**), so popular with visitors, lies at the centre of the medieval city of Cairo. Like all cities of the time it was protected by sturdy walls pierced by huge gates which were firmly closed at night. Large sections of the walls and some of the gates survive, for example at Bab el Futuh, Bab el Nasr and Bab Zuwayla, where climbing the gate towers is rewarded by fascinating views over the ancient, teeming streets. See **CAIRO-BUILDINGS & MONUMENTS 2**.

Cleopatra the Great (51-30 BC): The last of the Ptolemaic rulers (see **Ptolemies**), Cleopatra was married to two of her brothers before claiming the throne of Egypt for herself. Her liaisons with Julius Caesar and Mark Antony scandalized the Roman world. Otherwise an astute and capable ruler, her fatal error was to side with Mark Antony against Rome; the disastrous consequence of this alliance was defeat at the naval battle of Actium in 31 BC, following which Egypt was absorbed into the Roman Empire. In preference to the humiliation of being paraded in triumph, Cleopatra chose suicide.

Climate: Daytime temperatures generally vary from warm in the winter to very hot (over 50°C) in the summer, though prevailing breezes from the north normally prevent the heat from becoming unbearable. In Cairo it can be quite cold (under 10°C) during Dec. and Jan., and short, heavy rain showers are not uncommon. Luxor is normally a few degrees hotter than Cairo, and rain is rare, even in winter. Mornings and evenings can be cool, even in summer. From the end of Feb. until April, Egypt is visited by the khamsin, an unpleasant dust wind which can last from a few minutes to a few days.

Clothing: Comfortable shoes for sightseeing are an absolute essential; trainers can be useful for the rough terrain at archaeological sites. Bring also a sunhat or scarf, and sunglasses for protection against the sun. Layers of loose, comfortable clothing in natural fibres are the best choice for sightseeing, which often begins in the cool of the morning and continues into the heat of the day; a jacket or sweater for mornings and evenings is a 'must'. Bear in mind that Egypt is a Muslim country and extremely conservative – swimwear and shorts (on either sex) should not be worn anywhere except the swimming pool. As far as women (see **A-Z**) are concerned, miniskirts and sleeveless or low-cut garments are never acceptable street wear, and are guaranteed to attract unwelcome attention. In nightclubs, upmarket restaurants and on cruises it is customary for men to wear a jacket and tie at dinner, and a few places insist on suits.

Colossi of Memnon: These twin colossal statues, 18 m high, represent the deified pharaoh Amenhotep III (see **A-Z**), and are practically all that remains of his mortuary temple, destroyed by an earthquake in 27 BC. The resulting damage to the northern statue caused it for a time to 'sing' at dawn as the broken stone expanded. This phenomenon, which led ancient visitors to identify the statue with the legendary figure Memnon, stopped after repairs were made under Septimius Severus in the 3rdC AD. See **LUXOR-BUILDINGS & MONUMENTS 1**.

Complaints: All complaints should be handled with the utmost delicacy, as some Egyptians are very sensitive about even what is perceived as implied criticism. In a restaurant or hotel, asking discreetly for the manager usually produces results. Complaints about taxi or calèche drivers, boatmen, etc. are the province of the tourist police. Tour company representatives can help with really serious cases.

Consulates:
UK – 7 Ahmed Ragheb St, Garden City, tel: 3540850.
Eire – 3 Abu el Feda Tower, Zamalek, tel: 3408264.
Australia – Cairo Plaza, Corniche el Nil, Bulaq, tel: 777900.
Canada – 6 Mohammed Fahmi el Sayed St, Garden City, tel: 3543110.
New Zealand – Use the UK consulate.
USA – 5 Latin America St, Garden City, tel: 3557371.

Conversion Chart:

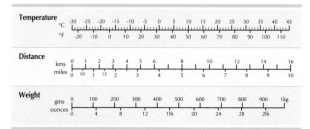

Coptic Museum: Mathaf el Qibti. Founded in 1910 as a home for Coptic antiquities from all over Egypt, the Coptic Museum is situated among pleasant gardens right in the heart of Old Cairo (see **A–Z**). The displays set out to trace the development of Coptic art, whose style spans the gap between Pharaonic and Graeco-Roman art and that of the Islamic period. The downstairs galleries house mainly architectural fragments such as carved stone friezes and frescoes, while upstairs are icons and manuscripts, textiles, woodwork, glass, metal and pottery. See **CAIRO-MUSEUMS 1, WALK 2.**

Crafts: Egypt has a flourishing craft tradition in many areas, including textiles and embroidery, carved and inlaid woodwork, leather, glass, pottery, stone carving, metalwork and jewellery. Most workshops, many of which are housed in historic buildings, welcome visitors. In recent years young artists have begun to adapt traditional techniques to modern ideas with fascinating results – their beautiful and original pieces still sell very reasonably in Cairo art galleries. See **CAIRO-ART GALLERIES, CRAFTS.**

Credit Cards: See Money.

Crime & Theft: Egypt is one of the safest places on earth for the visitor. Apart from crimes of passion, violent crime does not occur; there are no muggings. Although it makes sense to observe the usual safety precautions, it is safe to walk the streets at any hour – women may find the persistent verbal harassment from men threatening, but rape is virtually unknown. Pickpockets, however, do exist, and when out and about (particularly in crowded areas) you should take normal steps to protect your property. There is absolutely no need to carry large amounts of money or valuables around with you: hotels and cruise boats provide free safety-deposit boxes. See **Emergency Numbers**, **Insurance**, **Police**.

Currency: Egyptian currency is decimal, with 100 piastres (PT) to the Egyptian pound (LE). Notes come in denominations of LE 100, LE 20, LE 10, LE 5 and LE 1 and 50 PT, 25 PT, 10 PT and 5 PT. They are easily identified as their values are written in English as well as Arabic. Coins, which include 10 PT, 5 PT and 1 PT, have values written in Arabic-style numerals only. The millime, one-tenth of a piastre, is no longer a unit of currency, but prices may be given in millimes; thus one pound is LE 1, 100 PT or LE 1000. See **Alphabet & Numerals**, **Money**.

Customs: Egyptians are warm, friendly people who always take the time to greet one another; they find the brusque Western attitude rather rude, and courtesy, rather than punctuality, is the rule.
Remembering to smile, shake hands and say hello (*ahlan*) before plunging into the business on hand pays immense dividends in the treatment you receive. So does memorizing a few simple Arabic phrases: please (*min fadlak*) and thank you (*shukran*) are indispensable. Good morning when addressing someone is *sabah ilkheer* and the response is *sabah innur*; likewise, good afternoon (or evening) is *misaa ilkheer* and the answer *misaa innur*. Goodnight is *tisbah 'ala kheer* and goodbye *ma'assalaama*.
It is a common politeness to address people by their title and first name (Mr Adel, Dr Yasmin, etc.). If you wish to photograph someone, it is essential to ask permission first, as many people, especially women, see this as a violation of privacy. Physical displays of affection (kissing and hugging) between members of opposite sexes are not acceptable in public.

Customs Allowances:

Duty Free Into:	Cigarettes	or Cigars	or Tobacco	Spirits	Dessert Wine
EGYPT	200	25	200 g	1 *l*	or 1 *l*
UK	200	50	250 g	1 *l*	and 2 *l*

Duty-free shops are available both on arrival and departure, and within one month of arrival short-stay visitors may also make one visit to the duty-free shop in Gamaat Dowal el Arabeyya St in Mohandiseen or at Luxor airport.

Dendera: 60 km north of Luxor, Dendera was the cult centre of the goddess Hathor, cow-eared patroness of love, beauty and music. The lovely Graeco-Roman temple is a popular destination for excursions from Luxor. See **LUXOR-EXCURSION 1**.

Dentists: See Health.

Disabled Travellers: Facilities for disabled visitors are very limited, and bookings should be made well in advance. Transport can be a problem, due to the lack of adapted vehicles, and access at sites is also difficult. Hotels should be checked in advance concerning access in general, and to bathroom facilities in particular. Local people and hotel staff are always willing to help with particular problems. Chalfont Line Holidays, 4 Medway Parade, Perivale, Middlesex UB6 8HA, tel: 081-9973799, operates special package tours in Egypt for disabled visitors. In Cairo, ETAMS Tours, 4th floor, 99 Ramses St, Central Cairo, tel: 754721, has adapted vehicles and can organize programmes on request.

A–Z

Drinks: Egypt produces several types of wine (*nibit*), all reasonably priced, though of varying quality. Best known of the red wines is Omar Khayyam, while probably the best of the whites is Château Gianaclis. There is also a rosé, Rubis d'Egypte. Imported wines are prohibitively expensive. Most visitors enjoy Stella, the local beer, which is light, refreshing and inexpensive and comes in a bottle big enough for two. You can also find Stella Export – stronger and more expensive, it comes in smaller bottles – and a non-alcoholic version called Birell. Imported spirits are available, at a price. All the well-known brands of soft drinks (*haaga sa'a*) or their local equivalents, are available everywhere, though it is still hard to find diet versions. One of the real pleasures of Egypt is the variety of seasonal fresh fruit juices (*asir*), from orange and lemon to strawberry and sugar cane, but the commonest drinks are tea (*shai*) and coffee (*ahwa*). Tea is usually served very strong, without milk and ready-sugared, in small glasses. You can ask for it with a little sugar (*sukkar khafif*) or a lot (*sukkar ziada*), or you might like to try tea with peppermint (*shai bi na'na*). Coffee can be European style, but will usually be Arabic, strong and thick, served in a tiny cup. You need to tell the waiter how sweet you would like it: *saada* (no sugar), *arriha* (a little sugar), *mazbut* (medium) or *ziada* (sweet). Finally, for those with simpler tastes, there are several excellent local brands of mineral water (*mayya madiniyya*). See **Alcohol**.

Driving: On the whole, it is not advisable for short-stay visitors to attempt driving in Egypt; it is far simpler to hire a taxi or chauffeur-driven car. In Cairo the main problems are general chaos and lack of parking space. In the country the roads are often in a bad condition and there is danger from wandering animals and children. At night the roads are unlit and many accidents result from drivers being dazzled by oncoming traffic. If you do wish to bring your car into Egypt, you will need an International Driving Licence, car registration papers and a *carnet de passage* for exemption from import duty. You are also obliged to buy third-party insurance. Driving in Egypt is on the right. See **Accidents & Breakdowns**, **Car Hire**, **Petrol**.

Drugs: In their attempts to combat the problem of drug abuse, the Egyptian authorities take a very hard line. There is a mandatory sentence of death or life imprisonment for smuggling, trafficking or dealing in illegal drugs, including cannabis, and prison sentences of up to 25 years for those convicted of possession.

Eating Out: Eating out in Egypt is a national pastime, popular with all classes, and is one of the country's great pleasures: at about a quarter of European prices, indulgence is cheap! Cosmopolitan Cairo offers every type of cuisine imaginable, from roadside *fuul* stands and Wimpy bars to luxurious French brasseries and chic Japanese restaurants. In Luxor, the choice is more limited but nonetheless remarkable for such a small city. Many of the best-known restaurants are attached to the international hotels, where fixed-price lunch and dinner buffets are a popular choice.

In the **RESTAURANTS** topic sections of this guidebook 'Inexpensive' refers to restaurants serving main courses costing less than LE 10, 'Moderate', main courses LE 10-25, and 'Expensive', over LE 20. Restaurants in the latter category tend to be fairly formal and it is usual for men to wear a jacket and tie.

Restaurant: mat'aam; I'd/we'd like . . .: ayiz/ayzeen . . .

See **CAIRO-RESTAURANTS 1-4**, **LUXOR-RESTAURANTS 1 & 2**, **Food**.

Edfu: Edfu, 110 km south of Luxor, is famous for its temple, the most complete and best preserved in Egypt. Dedicated to Horus, the falcon-headed god of kingship, it was begun in 237 BC and completed 180 years later. The vast pylon represents Ptolemy XIII smiting the enemies of Egypt; touches of the original colour are still visible. Inside the peristyle court with its marvellous composite columns are two huge falcon statues, one in excellent condition. The inner rooms of the temple are equally well-preserved, even to the sanctuary which retains the original shrine and pedestal. In the ambulatory are some interesting reliefs of the battle between Horus and his wicked uncle Seth.

Egyptian Museum: Mathaf el Masri. To really see the Egyptian Museum's enormous collection of Pharaonic and Graeco-Roman artefacts takes several visits, but, if your time is limited, allow half a day to see the highlights. Built in 1900, the museum has two floors. The downstairs rooms are arranged in chronological order and house sculpture, sarcophagi and architectural fragments. Try not to miss the Old Kingdom sculptures such as the diorite statue of King Chephren (Room 42) and the lovely pair statue of Prince Rahotep and his wife Nofret (Room 32). Room 3, devoted to material from the reign of the heretic king Akhenaten (see **A-Z**), is also interesting. However, for most visitors the purpose of a visit to the Egyptian Museum is to see the fabled treasures of the boy king Tutankhamun (see **A-Z**) which occupy almost half of the upper floor (start at Room 45). Almost everything found in the tomb is displayed here, from the famous mask and jewellery to funerary equipment and the furniture, clothing, chariots and weaponry that he used in his everyday life. Perhaps most touching of all is the small display of his childhood toys. Next to Tutankhamun's four large gold shrines, take time to look into Room 3 which contains a spectacular collection of Pharaonic jewellery. The other upstairs galleries cover topics as varied as prehistory, papyri and writing materials, coffins, tools and pottery. Of particular interest are the tomb models in Rooms 27, 32 and 37, which are perfect miniatures of ancient houses, ships and workshops. The display of royal mummies, which was closed under Sadat (see **A-Z**), has now reopened and Room 53 has a good collection of mummified animals. All travel agents offer guided tours of the Egyptian Museum. See **CAIRO-MUSEUMS 1**.

El Alamein: Situated on Egypt's Mediterranean coast approximately 100 km west of Alexandria, El Alamein was the scene of intensive fighting during World War II. Culminating in a decisive Allied victory in 1942, the battle marked the turning point of the North African campaign. Today, three war cemeteries – Commonwealth, German and Italian – mark the battlefields, and there is a small museum with maps, models and displays relating the story of the struggle. See **Events**.

El Azhar: In 1983, El Azhar celebrated its thousandth anniversary as a teaching university, making it the oldest such institution in the world. Begun in 970 as the congregational mosque for the Fatimid (see **A-Z**) city of Cairo, it soon established itself as a centre of learning; today it remains the most respected theological centre of the Islamic world. The present structure is a jumble of styles and periods, the oldest parts being the central court and the sanctuary which date from the Fatimid period, though the decorative elements are later additions. The two Mamluk (see **A-Z**) madrasas (see **A-Z**) just inside the main entrance are worth visiting for their intricately decorated mihrabs. The three minarets, which also date from this period, offer fascinating views over the medieval city. See **CAIRO-BUILDINGS & MONUMENTS 2**.

Electricity: 220V AC: two-pin round plugs. Power cuts are not uncommon, but large hotels usually have an emergency generator.

El Kab: Lying 85 km south of Luxor on the main road to Aswan, El Kab – ancient Nekheb – was once the capital of the third nome (province) of Upper Egypt (see **A-Z**) and the cult centre of the vulture goddess Nekhbet. Its massive mudbrick city walls, 11 m thick, are the first thing to catch the eye as you approach by road. Although little remains inside, they are worth a climb to get an idea of the scale of an ancient Egyptian town. In the cliffs behind the town are many rock-cut tombs dating to the Middle and New kingdoms; four of these are open and are worth visiting for their interesting texts and paintings. Further on, in the desert, are small temples and chapels of the New Kingdom and Ptolemaic (see **A-Z**) periods.

Emergency Numbers:
Cairo – El Salam International Hospital, Corniche el Nil, Maadi, tel: 3638050.
Anglo-American Hospital, Zohoreya, Zamalek, tel: 3418630.
Luxor – Dr Bolok, El Khor St, tel: 382945.
Tourist police offices:
Cairo – 5 Adly St, Central Cairo, tel: 912644
Luxor – Tourist Bazaar, Corniche el Nil, tel: 382120.

Esna: Situated 55 km south of Luxor, Esna was once famous as a tex-tile centre, and it is still a good place to shop for *galabeyas*, tablecloths,

etc. Most visitors, however, only make a short stop to see the remains of the Roman Temple of Khnum. Sited about 9 m below ground level in the middle of the town and increasingly threatened by rising damp, only the hypostyle hall survives. Dedicated to the ram-headed creator god Khnum, it is best known for its 24 huge columns with their very fine composite capitals. There are also some interesting reliefs of Roman emperors before various gods. Its chief interest to Egyptologists lies in the texts, which give details of the liturgical calendar.

Events:

January: International Book Fair, Medinet Nasr Exhibition Grounds, Heliopolis, Cairo.
February: International Bridge Tournament, Cairo; International Fishing Tournament, Hurghada.
March: Spring Flower Show, Botanical Gardens, Cairo; International Trade Fair, Medinet Nasr Exhibition Grounds, Heliopolis, Cairo.
September: International Theatre Festival, Ismailia, folk performers from around the world; The Pharoahs' Rally, now ranked as one of the world's top rallies, this 11-day, 4700 km race through Egypt's deserts attracts a high-calibre field; Battle of El Alamein commemoration.
December: Cairo International Film Festival, two weeks of the latest international releases and established classics, shown at various venues around the city (see **Cinema**).

Farouk I (1920-65): Egypt's last king, Farouk ascended the throne in 1936, but was forced to abdicate following the Revolution of 1952.

Fathy, Hassan (1902-89): The architect Hassan Fathy was one of the pioneers of the Egyptian arts and crafts revival of the 1930s and 40s. Rejecting imported building techniques, he returned to the ancient practice of building in mudbrick, drawing on Pharaonic and peasant traditions to create a uniquely Egyptian style that was at the same time cheap, easy and quick to build. See **LUXOR-BUILDINGS & MONUMENTS 2**, **Garagos**.

Fatimids: Descendants of Fatima, the Prophet Mohammed's

daughter, the Fatimids were Shi'ite Muslims from Tunisia who con-
quered Egypt in 969 and founded the city of Cairo. After a short period
of brilliance, the dynasty weakened and finally collapsed in 1171. The
Fatimid architectural legacy can be seen in the mosques of El Azhar
(see **A-Z**) and El Hakim and in Cairo's ancient gates and City Walls (see
A-Z).

Fayyum: The Fayyum is a delightful semi-oasis region situated 70 km southwest of Cairo. A popular day trip destination for Cairenes and tourists alike, Fayyum's attractions include archaeological monuments as well as the picturesque sights of the countryside. See **CAIRO-EXCURSION 3**.

Feluccas: Feluccas are the elegant sailing boats seen on the Nile in Cairo and Luxor. They can be hired by the hour in Cairo from landings near the Meridien Hotel in Garden City or near the Good Shot in Maadi, and in Luxor along the Corniche. You will need to negotiate a price – check the tariff at the tourist information office first. A felucca sail is a very relaxing way to enjoy the view – copy the locals and take a picnic along. Some adventurous souls like to travel by felucca between Luxor and Aswan, a journey of several days, depending on the wind. This can be arranged through some tour operators, or you can negotiate a deal with a local boatman.

Festivals & Calendars: There are three calendars in use in Egypt – the Gregorian, Islamic and Coptic. The Gregorian is the normal Western calendar, which is used for all secular purposes. The Islamic calendar is lunar, with 12 months of 29 or 30 days, and dates from the Hegira, the flight of the Prophet and his companions from Mecca to Medina in AD 622. Used mainly for religious purposes, it is 11 days shorter than the Western year, so Islamic festivals fall on a different day each year. Important months are Ramadan (see **A-Z**), the month of fasting, and Dhu'l-Hijja, during which the Pilgrimage to Mecca takes place. Important Islamic festivals include Islamic New Year (Ras el San'a), the Prophet's Birthday (Mulid el Nabi), Eid el Fitr, the feast at the end of Ramadan, and Eid el Adha commemorating the sacrifice of Abraham. All of these are public holidays.

The Coptic calendar is solar and comprises 12 months of 30 days, plus 5 extra days (6 in leap years). It is believed to derive from the ancient Egyptian calendar and is still used by farmers. Known as the Calendar of the Martyrs, it dates from AD 284 and commemorates the persecution of Christians under the emperor Diocletian. Principal Coptic feasts include Coptic New Year (11-12 Sep.), Christmas (7 Jan.), Easter, Pentecost, the Apostles' Feast (12 July) and the Feast of the Virgin (22 Aug.). None is a public holiday.

Both Christians and Muslims celebrate *mulids*, festivals in honour of local saints and holy men. A typical example is the *mulid* of Abu el Haggag, a holy man buried in the mosque inside Luxor Temple, held annually in Luxor on 14 Shaaban, two weeks before Ramadan. It is celebrated with parades, sideshows and entertainments as well as prayers and Qur'an readings. See **Public Holidays**.

Fishing: Good sport fishing is available on the Nile, in the lakes, and along the Mediterranean and Red Sea coasts. International tournaments are held at Hurghada (see **Events**). In Luxor, fishing tackle can be hired from the Luxor Sheraton Hotel – contact Guest Relations.

Folk Music & Dance: Egypt has a very rich tradition of folk music and dance, preserved by companies such as the Reda Troupe and National Troupe who perform regularly at the Balloon Theatre in Cairo.

Arabic music fans should look out for performances by the Arabic Music Troupe, Om Khalsoum Ensemble or Folkloric Orchestra of Egypt; venues include the Opera House (see **A–Z**), Sayed Darwish Concert Hall and Goumhoreya Theatre. Check local press for details. See **Newspapers**, **What's On**.

Food: Egyptian cooking has much in common with the cuisines of the Mediterranean and Middle East, its mainstays being simple grilled meat dishes such as kebab and kofta, usually served with rice. Pasta is also very popular and is frequently served in dishes like *koshari*, mixed rice, lentils, macaroni and chickpeas served with crisply-fried onions and

hot tomato sauce. The staple of the masses since time immemorial has been the brown bean, *fuul*, which is served stewed as a breakfast dish or made into delicious deep-fried patties called *tameyya*. Another dish believed to date from Pharaonic times is *molokheyya*, a green leafy vegetable made into a rich, garlicky soup; it is often served with rabbit or chicken. Another speciality is grilled pigeon stuffed with rice or wheat, and the excellent lake and sea fish and Red Sea shrimp should not be missed. A meal usually starts with *mezze* – a selection of small dishes including salads, yoghurt, tahina (ground sesame paste), olives, cheese and *mahshi* (stuffed vegetables such as courgettes and vine leaves). These are served with *aish baladi*, flat local bread – in Luxor, try *aish shamsi*, a slightly bitter version leavened in the sun. Desserts tend to the sweet and sticky, with endless varieties of syrupy cakes like baklava, *basbusa* and *konafa*. *Mahalabeyya* is a kind of blancmange, and there is also *om ali*, a rich milky bread pudding full of nuts and raisins. Those with simpler tastes will enjoy the fresh seasonal fruits which include dates, figs, melons, strawberries, bananas and oranges. See **CAIRO-RESTAURANTS 1-4**, **LUXOR-RESTAURANTS 1 & 2**, **Eating Out**.

Fortress of Babylon: Built in AD 130 by the emperor Trajan, the remains of the Roman/Byzantine Fortress of Babylon lie around and under the Coptic Museum (see **A–Z**) and the Hanging Church (see **A–Z**) in the heart of Old Cairo (see **A–Z**). Despite flooding it is still possible to see the old water gate from which the last Byzantine (see **A–Z**) governor escaped during the Arab invasion of AD 641. See **CAIRO-BUILDINGS & MONUMENTS 1, WALK 2**.

Garagos: For a close-up view of village life, visit Garagos, a small village about 30 km north of Luxor. The site of an early development project by Franciscan monks, Garagos boasts a pottery workshop designed by Hassan Fathy (see **A–Z**), as well as a church, school and hospital, all of which welcome visitors. See **LUXOR-EXCURSION 1**.

Giza: The Giza plateau, just west of the city of Cairo, was an important necropolis during the Old Kingdom, and is the site of the Pyramids and Sphinx. See **CAIRO-WALK 1**.

Gods: Egyptian religion is very complex and trying to identify the various deities can be very confusing. However, with a little practice it is not impossible to recognize the principal gods and goddesses. Horus, the god of kingship, is represented as a hawk-headed man; his wife Hathor, goddess of love and beauty, is shown as a woman with cows' ears, sometimes wearing horns and a sun disc. Ptah, the creator god of Memphis (see **A–Z**), wears a blue skull cap; his wife is the lioness-headed goddess of destruction, Sekhmet. Osiris, the Lord of the Underworld, is always coloured black or green; he wears the wrappings of a mummy and a distinctive tall crown. His wife is Isis, goddess of magic, whose symbol is the throne. Another protector of the dead is Anubis, the jackal-headed god of embalming. The patron of learning, Thoth, is represented

either as an ibis or an ape. The deity of Thebes
(see **A–Z**), Amun, wears a crown with double plumes; Mut, his wife,
has a vulture headdress and their son Khonsu the lunar disc and crescent. And everybody can recognize Bes, the jolly dwarf god!

Great Pyramid: Built for the pharaoh Cheops (see A–Z) around
2570 BC and the largest in Egypt, the Great Pyramid is 137 m high and
contains over a quarter of a million cubic metres of stone. The chief
feature of the interior is the grand gallery, one of the miracles of ancient
engineering. At 47 m long and 8.5 m high, with a magnificent cor-
belled roof, it leads to the undecorated burial chamber in the heart of
the pyramid. See **CAIRO-BUILDINGS & MONUMENTS 1, WALK 1**.

Guides: All licensed guides are competent professionals, normally
with a university background, who have passed stringent historical and

language examinations. They should not be confused with the unoffi-
cial guides who loiter around museums and monuments. Guides (*mur-
shideen*) can be booked through travel agents. See **Tourist Information**,
Tours.

Hanging Church: El Mu'allaqa. Founded in the 7thC, this church is built over the bastions of the Fortress of Babylon (see **A-Z**) in Old Cairo, hence its unusual name. Rebuilt several times, the present structure dates mainly from the 11thC. It is notable for its fine sanctuary screen of carved cedarwood inlaid with ivory. See **CAIRO-BUILDINGS & MONUMENTS 1, WALK 2**.

Hatshepsut (c.1498-1483 BC): After usurping the throne from the young Tuthmosis III (see **A-Z**), Egypt's famous female pharaoh's short reign seems to have been one of peace and prosperity, and she left several beautiful monuments, one of which is her mortuary temple, located at Deir el Bahari on the West Bank at Luxor (see **LUXOR-BUILDINGS & MONUMENTS 1**).

Health: Unless you are arriving from an area infected with cholera or yellow fever, there are no required vaccinations for Egypt. However, immunization against typhoid, cholera, tetanus and polio is considered advisable. Certain parts of Egypt are malarial during the summer, and your doctor may recommend prophylactic tablets. Hepatitis is endemic; a gamma globulin injection just before departure will increase resistance. Almost every visitor gets an attack of 'gippy tummy'; symptoms – violent vomiting and diarrhoea – are alarming but seldom serious. The best cure consists of bed rest and liquids only for 24 hr followed by a simple diet of boiled rice and plain toast for a day or two. Rehydration salts (available locally under the brand name Rehydrin) are extremely helpful. Medication is only necessary if symptoms persist after 48 hr. There are some excellent local remedies; a doctor or pharmacist will advise. Prevention, however, is better than cure, and short-stay visitors are usually advised to avoid uncooked food and drink only bottled water. Sunburn and heat stroke can also be a problem, and suitable precautions, including a sunhat and appropriate sun screen, should be taken. During hot weather it is important to drink plenty of liquids to prevent dehydration. The very dusty atmosphere can cause problems for asthmatics and people with allergies, and coughs and sore throats are common. Avoid swimming or paddling in canals, the habitat of the unpleasant and potentially lethal bilharzia parasite. Mosquito bites can be unpleasant; cover up in the evenings and use an insect repellent. Rabies is endemic; do not touch any animals, and if scratched or bitten seek medical advice. Normal precautions should be taken against sexually-transmitted diseases; condoms (brand name Tops) are available from chemists. Remember to bring adequate supplies of prescribed medication; if you regularly use a particular medicine, it is a good precaution to ask your doctor for its pharmaceutical name, as it will probably be sold under a different brand name in Egypt. Certain products, such as contact lens fluid, can be difficult to obtain; again, take adequate supplies.

Cairo has a number of excellent hospitals and all modern medical services; facilities in Luxor are more limited, but adequate. Most doctors, dentists and pharmacists speak English, and many have trained in Britain or the USA; hotels and tour company representatives can help find a suitable practitioner. Medical bills must *always* be settled in cash, and hospitals require a substantial cash deposit on admission; they do not accept medical insurance. See **Emergency Numbers**, **Insurance**.

High Dam: Completed in 1970, the Aswan High Dam is a miracle of modern engineering. 3.6 km in length, it has created Lake Nasser, a huge reservoir 500 km long. This has enabled perennial irrigation as well as the production of hydro-electric power. Although the dam has had undoubted benefits for Egypt, it has been a mixed blessing in terms of the rise in the water table, among whose effects are the destruction of monuments and increased salinity in the Nile Delta. See LUXOR-EXCURSION 2.

History: As far as the ancient Egyptians were concerned, their history began around 3200 BC with the unification of the two lands of Upper and Lower Egypt (see **A-Z**) under the semi-mythical king Narmer, or Menes. Later the priest Manetho divided the country's past into eras called Kingdoms presided over by Dynasties of ruling families and separated by Intermediate Periods. During the Old Kingdom (c.2700-2200 BC) the capital was at Memphis (see **A-Z**). This was the Pyramid Age, when divine kings ruled over a state designed to serve their needs.

Following a period of unrest known as the First Intermediate Period, the Middle Kingdom (c.2000-1800 BC) was a time of rebuilding and consolidation under new rulers from Thebes (modern Luxor). The Second Intermediate Period saw an invasion of Asiatic herders known as the Hyksos, who occupied the northern part of the country until expelled by the Thebans around 1780 BC. This marked the beginning of the New Kingdom under the remarkable Eighteenth Dynasty, whose members included the female pharaoh Hatshepsut (see **A-Z**), the heretic king Akhenaten (see **A-Z**) and his son Tutankhamun (see **A-Z**). This family was succeeded by the Nineteenth Dynasty, the Ramessides, who produced some equally notable personalities such as Seti I (see **A-Z**) and his son Ramesses II (see **A-Z**). The New Kingdom finally collapsed around 1070 BC and was followed by a period of decline known as the Third Intermediate Period. The invasion of the Persian Cambyses in 525 BC marked the beginning of the Late Period and the incorporation of Egypt into the Achaemenid Empire. Subsequently, Alexander the Great (see **A-Z**) defeated the Persians and took possession of Egypt in 332 BC. Following his death, Egypt passed into the hands of the Ptolemies (see **A-Z**), the last of whom was the legendary Cleopatra the Great (see **A-Z**). After Cleopatra's defeat by the Romans (see **A-Z**) at the Battle of Actium in 31 BC, Egypt was incorporated into the Roman Empire, later the Byzantine Empire; Christianity (see **A-Z**) became the official religion under Theodosius in the 4thC AD. However, in 641, Arab forces under the general Amr ibn el 'As defeated the Byzantines (see **A-Z**) and Egypt became an Islamic country. Ruled in turn by a succession of Muslim dynasties, notably the Fatimids (see **A-Z**), Ayyubids and Mamluks (see **A-Z**), in 1517 it fell to the Ottomans (see **A-Z**) and became part of their empire. After the Napoleonic invasion of 1798-1801, the new Viceroy of Egypt, Mohammed Ali (see **A-Z**), declared himself independent of the Ottoman Empire and went on to found his own dynasty. Independence, however, was curtailed by the British occupation of 1882, and in 1914 Egypt was declared a British protectorate. In 1922 it nominally became an independent monarchy, but a mere 30 years later the last of Mohammed Ali's line, King Farouk (see **A-Z**), was deposed in the bloodless Revolution led by the Free Officers, among them Gamal Abdel Nasser (see **A-Z**) and Anwar Sadat (see **A-Z**).

Ibn Tulun Mosque: Built in the 9thC by the Abbasid Governor of Egypt, Ahmed ibn Tulun, this excellent example of a congregational mosque is Cairo's oldest complete Islamic monument. Since the Abbasid capital was at Baghdad, Mesopotamian influence is much in evidence in the architecture, particularly in the use of stucco decoration and in the unusual spiral minaret. Striking in its elegant simplicity, this mosque should be on every visitor's itinerary. See **CAIRO-BUILDINGS & MONUMENTS 2**.

Insurance: A comprehensive travel insurance policy – preferably one which provides for emergency repatriation – is essential for visitors to Egypt. See **Crime & Theft**, **Health**.

Islam: The faith of Islam, which means submission, was first preached by the Prophet Muhammad who lived in Mecca, Saudi Arabia, during the 7thC AD. Adherents of the faith, known as Muslims, believe in the same God as the Jews and Christians; they accept the Old Testament prophets and also Jesus – but as another prophet, not the Son of God. The Muslim holy book, which was divinely revealed to the Prophet, is called the Qur'an. Following the death of the Prophet, the spiritual leadership of the Islamic community passed to a series of caliphs. It was one hotly-contested challenge to this position that created the split between the Shi'ites, who believe that spiritual leadership rightly belongs to the Prophet's descendants, and the Sunnis, who claim to uphold the Prophet's own tradition. 90% of Egyptians are Sunni Muslims. There is no priesthood in Islam; there are, however, religious scholars who give legal and theological opinions, and most mosques have an imam to lead the prayer. All Muslims must observe the five major principles or 'pillars' of Islam. The first of these is the affirmation that there is only one God and that the Prophet Muhammad is the Messenger of God. The second is prayer, which must be performed five times a day facing Mecca; Fri. noon is a special time of prayer when men congregate at the mosque. The third is almsgiving. The fourth is fasting during the holy month of Ramadan (see **A-Z**), and the fifth is, if circumstances permit, to make the Pilgrimage to Mecca. To perform the Pilgrimage is the burning ambition of most ordinary Egyptians and a man who has achieved it proudly bears the title Hagg (a woman, Hagga); in Upper Egypt, pilgrims' houses often have colourful wall paintings of Mecca to commemorate the occasion. Muslims also observe dietary restrictions forbidding the consumption of pork and alcohol. See **Festivals & Calendars**, **Mosques**.

Islamic Cairo: The first Islamic settlement in the Cairo area was a garrison town called Fustat established to the northeast of the Fortress of Babylon (see **A-Z**) following the defeat of the Byzantines (see **A-Z**) in 641 AD. Subsequent development continued in a northeasterly direction – first, in the 9thC, was Ahmed ibn Tulun's city of El Qatai where his mosque still stands (see **Ibn Tulun Mosque**). Next came the Fatimid (see **A-Z**) city of El Qahira (Cairo), many of whose monuments survive within its massive walls. In the 12thC, Saladin (see **A-Z**) continued to extend and fortify, building the Citadel (see **A-Z**). Further expansion took place under the Mamluks (see **A-Z**), and later the Ottomans (see **A-Z**) added their distinctive contribution to the plethora of architectural styles. An excellent model in the Military Museum (see **CAIRO-MUSEUMS 2**) at the Citadel shows the city's successive stages of development. Islamic monuments are generally accessible from early morning to sunset, but at less well-known sites it may take time to locate the custodian. Some buildings can be visited for free, but there is usually a charge at more popular monuments; if asked for money, make sure you receive a ticket in exchange.

Karnak: This enormous temple complex, dedicated to the Theban deities Amun, Mut and Khonsu, contains monuments spanning 2000 years of Egyptian history. There are two Sound & Light shows (see **A-Z**)

every evening; check the programme for times and days of English-language presentations. See **LUXOR-BUILDINGS & MONUMENTS 2**, **WALK 2**.

Kerdassa: Situated just outside Cairo, this weavers' village, famous for rugs, shawls and tapestries, once served the caravan routes to the oases.

Khan el Khalili Bazaar: Located in and around a 14thC caravanserai, Khan el Khalili is Cairo's main bazaar area and home to many traditional craft workshops. See **CAIRO-CRAFTS**, **SHOPPING 1**.

Kom Ombo: 170 km south of Luxor by road, the ruined temple of Kom Ombo is picturesquely set among fields beside the Nile. Dating from the Graeco-Roman period, it is unique in that it is dedicated to two gods, Horus the Elder and the crocodile-headed god Sobek; each god had his own sanctuary and suite of cult rooms. In ancient times Kom Ombo was a centre of healing, and this is reflected in the famous relief of medical instruments. Look out, too, for the games and pictures scratched on the pavement by pilgrims awaiting consultations. Another point of interest is the well, which may once have housed the sacred crocodiles whose mummified remains are now kept in a small chapel.

Language: Arabic is the official language. Many people also speak some English or French. It is well worth the effort to learn a few words of Arabic as your attempts will be warmly appreciated.
Do you speak English?: bititkallam ingliizi?
See **Customs**.

Laundries: All but the smallest hotels have a laundry service, and the larger ones offer dry-cleaning (*tandiif 'ala naasif*) as well. Service is usually fast, good and excellent value, but be careful with delicate garments. In Cairo, neighbourhood laundries and cleaners offer the same service more cheaply, and in Luxor the big hotels provide facilities for non-residents. Cheaper still is to do your own washing and take it to the local ironing shop – ask for the *makwagi*.

Lost Property: The first step is to contact the relevant authorities wherever you lost your property (airport, station, bus or taxi company, etc.). Your tour company representative or hotel should be able to help with this. If the loss is serious you must also inform the tourist police, especially if you need to claim on your travel insurance. Lost credit cards and traveller's cheques must be reported to the relevant companies immediately – make sure before leaving home that you have the telephone numbers with you. Lost passports must be reported to your consulate, which can issue replacement documents. Finally, don't give up hope – Egyptians are extraordinarily honest, and it's amazing how often seemingly irretrievably lost items find their way home. See **Consulates**, **Insurance**.

Luxor Museum: A delightful small museum, cool and modern, with a well-displayed collection of antiquities from the Luxor area, including some of the finds from the tomb of Tutankhamun (see **A-Z**). Particularly interesting pieces include sculpted heads of Sesostris III and Amenhotep III (see **A-Z**), a fine black basalt statue of Tuthmosis III (see **A-Z**) and blocks from Akhenaten's sun temple at Karnak (see **A-Z**). See **LUXOR-BUILDINGS & MONUMENTS 2, WALK 1**.

Luxor Temple: Ma'bad Luxor. Situated on the Corniche in the heart

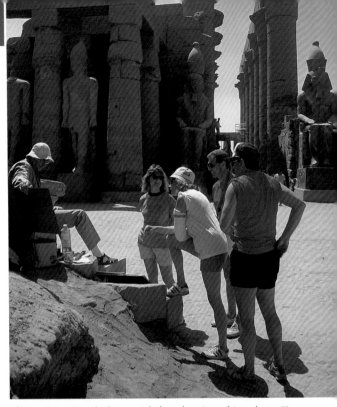

of Luxor, Luxor Temple dates mainly from the reigns of Amenhotep III (see **A-Z**) and Ramesses II (see **A-Z**). Open until late, the evening is the best time to take a quiet stroll when the crowds have gone and the floodlights enhance the delicate reliefs. See **LUXOR-BUILDINGS & MONU-MENTS 2, WALK 1**.

Madrasas: The madrasa is a special type of mosque which also serves as a theological college; it is characterized by having a central court surrounded by four halls to accommodate the teaching of the four schools of Sunni law. Introduced by Saladin (see **A-Z**) in an attempt to suppress Fatimid Shi'ism, some good examples of madrasas include those built by the Mamluk Sultans Hassan (see **Sultan Hassan Madrasa**), Qalawun (see **A-Z**) and Qaitbey (see **A-Z**).

Mamluks: For much of the Middle Ages, Egypt was dominated by the rule of the Mamluks, freed slaves who, having fought their way to power, were determined to hang on to it by any means possible. Two Mamluk groups held sway during this time: the Bahris (1250-1382), whose leaders included Qalawun and Hassan, were mainly Turks, and the Burgis (1383-1517), among them Sultan Qaitbey, who were of Circassian origin. Often a period of horrific violence, the Mamluk era was nonetheless a golden age for architecture and the arts, and some of Cairo's most glorious monuments date from this time. Despite their defeat at the hands of the Ottomans (see **A-Z**) in 1517, the Mamluks continued to play an influential role in Egyptian politics until 1811, when the last of their leaders were massacred by Mohammed Ali (see **A-Z**).

Manial Palace: Saray el Manial. Built in 1901 for King Farouk's uncle, in an interesting blend of European and Oriental styles, the original furnishings and collections are well-preserved and make for a fascinating visit. The extensive gardens, now housing the Club Med Hotel, are a pleasant place to escape the bustle of Cairo. See **CAIRO-BUILDINGS & MONUMENTS 3, MUSEUMS 2**.

Markets: You don't have to look far for a market (*suq*) in Cairo – local markets selling fruit and vegetables, household goods and clothing are everywhere. There are also specialized markets, such as Muski (near Khan el Khalili) for clothes, Shubra for vegetables and Embaba for the camel market (Fri. and Sun. am only). In Luxor, the daily market in Suq St caters for both tourists and locals; on Tue. am there is also a livestock market at El Hibel village, east of the town. See **CAIRO-SHOPPING 1-3, LUXOR-SHOPPING, Bargaining, Shopping**.

Mastabas: Deriving its name from the Arabic word for 'bench', a mastaba is a tomb consisting of one or more underground burial chambers and a low rectangular superstructure containing suites of rooms serving the cult of the deceased. Normally these would include an offering chapel with a false door to allow the spirit of the departed to emerge and partake of offerings. Typical tombs of the Old Kingdom, the best-known mastabas are at Sakkara (see **A-Z**); belonging to Fifth and Sixth Dynasty nobles, they are famous for their finely-detailed reliefs of everyday life.

Meal Times: Although hotels and tourist restaurants accommodate Western meal times, Egyptians have quite different customs which are worth knowing should you receive an invitation. Lunch, the main meal of the day, is usually taken around 1500-1600, dinner around 2400. During Ramadan (see **A-Z**), there are two meals a day – *iftar*, just after sunset, and *sohour*, an hour or two before dawn. If invited to dine at an Egyptian home, it is usual to bring a gift such as flowers – not alcohol.

Memphis: Of the city of Memphis, first capital of Egypt, very little now remains to interest the average visitor. There is, however, an open-air museum containing examples of statuary found at the site; an extra ticket is needed for photography. See **CAIRO-BUILDINGS & MONUMENTS 1, EXCURSION 1.**

Metro: Cairo's new Metro is fast, clean and, with tickets starting at 25 PT, cheap; trains run every few minutes 0530-0100. At present only one line is operational, running south from Ramses Sq. via Old Cairo to Maadi and Helwan, but east-west lines are planned for the near future. A bonus for female travellers is that the first carriage of every train is a 'harem car' for women only. Not to be confused with the above is the Heliopolis Metro, a tram system linking Cairo's city centre with the northeastern suburbs.

Mohammed Ali (1769-1849): Following the defeat of Napoleon (see **A-Z**) in 1801, Mohammed Ali, formerly an Albanian mercenary, was appointed the Ottoman Viceroy of Egypt. Having consolidated his position by massacring the remaining Mamluk (see **A-Z**) leaders, he went on to found a dynasty that lasted until 1952, the last in the line being Farouk (see **A-Z**). Mohammed Ali was a great innovator, and was committed to the modernization of Egypt; during his long reign (1805-48) he introduced many of today's cash crops such as cotton and sugar cane. His most striking monument is the Mohammed Ali Mosque (see **A-Z**).

Mohammed Ali Mosque: Dominating the Cairo skyline from its position atop the Citadel (see **A-Z**), the mosque of Mohammed Ali (see **A-Z**) with its twin pencil minarets presents an unmistakably Ottoman silhouette. Begun in 1824, it is also known as the Alabaster Mosque, from the lavish amount of that stone used in its construction. It is entered through an open court with an ornate ablution fountain and an equally fancy clock; the latter was a gift from Louis Philippe in exchange for the Luxor Temple obelisk now gracing Place de la Concorde in Paris. The domed interior is impressive in scale. Mohammed Ali's tomb is just inside the entrance on the right. The Mohammed Ali Mosque is included on many tour itineraries. See **CAIRO-WALK 3.**

Monasteries: Organized communities of Christian monks existed in Egypt as early as the 3rdC. Some of the oldest functioning monasteries are situated in the Wadi Natrun (see **A-Z**) near Cairo; there are also excursions to St. Catherine's Monastery (see **A-Z**) in Sinai. From Luxor it is possible to visit the now abandoned 6thC Monastery of St. Simeon at Aswan (see **LUXOR-EXCURSION 2**). Monasteries are normally closed Fri., Sun., religious holidays and during Holy Week.

Money: The currency in Egypt is the Egyptian pound (LE), which is a soft currency usable only within Egypt. All payments and purchases in Egypt must be made in Egyptian pounds. These have to be purchased at the official rate from banks; the exchange rate is published daily. The illegal exchange of money is a criminal offence. When changing money or traveller's cheques, ensure that your receipt is properly stamped and keep it safe – you will need to produce it if, for example, you wish to settle your hotel bill in Egyptian pounds or to extend your visa. You will also need it if you wish to re-exchange Egyptian currency on departure. No more than LE 20 can be imported or exported, so theoretically Egyptian pounds can be re-exchanged at the airport banks on departure, provided receipts are produced. In practice, however, these banks never seem to have any hard currency, so the hapless visitor is left with handfuls of worthless notes. The wise approach is to run down your supply of Egyptian pounds prior to departure – a good tip is to save small notes and traveller's cheques for the end of your trip so you can exchange only what you are sure you will spend. If you bring hard currency (not traveller's cheques) into Egypt you must declare this on arrival and complete a Currency Declaration Form; if you do not, any remaining cash is liable to confiscation upon departure.

Branches of the big national banks such as National Bank of Egypt and Banque du Caire can be found in all main streets and large hotels. Travel agents such as Thomas Cook and American Express also have exchange facilities. The exchange rate, set daily, is the same everywhere. You will be charged a small commission when exchanging traveller's cheques, and will need to produce your passport. It is usually easier to use the banks in hotels, as the procedure is less complicated and the hours more convenient. Many hotels in Cairo have 24-hr

banks, and in Luxor, hotel banks are normally open 0800-2100.
Businesses that regularly deal with foreigners, e.g. travel agents, large
hotels and restaurants, car-hire firms and a small but increasing number
of shops now accept the major credit cards, but their use is by no
means universal, so make sure you have an alternative source of
finance. American Express branches in Cairo and Luxor will advance
cash to their cardholders. This facility is also available at certain banks
to holders of other cards; it can be a useful source of emergency funds,
so obtain addresses from your card company before departure. Lost or
stolen cards must be reported immediately to the local police and to
the card company – remember to take the telephone number with you
just in case. See **Currency**.

Mosques: There are two basic types of mosques; the local mosque
(*masgid*) and the congregational mosque (*gami'a*). In their simplest
form, both types comprise an entrance, a courtyard or prayer hall and a
sanctuary area; the chief difference is in size, as between a parish
church and a cathedral. Since Muslims face Mecca during prayer, the
mosque must be oriented in this direction. The wall facing Mecca is
called the kibla, and is distinguished by a niche, often elaborately decorated, called the mihrab. Beside it is the pulpit (*minbar*) from which
the Fri. sermon is delivered. Muslims pray five times a day (dawn,
noon, mid-afternoon, sunset and night); at these times the faithful are
called to prayer from the tall towers known as minarets. The purpose of
a mosque is to provide a clean, quiet place for prayer and meditation
away from the distractions of the street. Decoration, therefore, is kept to
a minimum. In accordance with Islamic principles forbidding represen-
tational art, it normally consists of geometric or floral patterns, or calli-
graphic inscriptions of verses from the Qur'an. Most Egyptian mosques
welcome visitors, who should observe certain courtesies. Both sexes
should dress conservatively (you may be asked to put on a loose robe)
and women should cover their hair. Shoes must either be removed or
covered with special overshoes. It is best not to visit mosques during
prayer times, but if you find yourself in a mosque where people are
praying it is usually all right to stay provided you do not walk in front of
anyone. On Fri. it is best to complete all visits before the noon prayer.

Mukhtar, Mahmud (1891-1934): Widely regarded as Egypt's national sculptor, Mukhtar pioneered the Egyptian artistic revival of the 1930s and 40s. Combining the monumentality of Pharaonic sculpture with the dynamism of Egyptian folk art, works such as the *Renaissance of Egypt* at University Sq. (see **CAIRO-BUILDINGS & MONUMENTS 3**) and the Saad Zaghloul Monument near the Opera House give eloquent and powerful testimony to the spirit of Egyptian Nationalism. The small Mahmud Mukhtar Museum (see **CAIRO-MUSEUMS 2**) in Cairo is well worth a visit.

Musafirkhana Palace: Saray Musafirkhana. Formerly a royal guest-house, the Musafirkhana Palace now accommodates artists' studios. A typical 18thC palace, recent conservation work has restored many of its fine features to their former glory. See **CAIRO-CRAFTS**.

Museum of Islamic Art: Mathaf el Islami. Magnificent collection covering the entire history of Islamic art, with pieces from all over the Muslim world. The museum is particularly rich in architectural elements taken from old buildings in Cairo including decorative glass, stone and woodwork. There is also a fine collection of textiles and carpets and displays of metalwork, ceramics, illuminated manuscripts and bookbindings. See **CAIRO-MUSEUMS 2**.

Napoleon (1769-1821): In an attempt to gain control of the sea route to India, the French Emperor Napoleon invaded Egypt in 1798. Although he successfully crushed Egyptian resistance at the Battle of the Pyramids, the British under Nelson destroyed his fleet at Aboukir, and in 1801 the French were obliged to withdraw. However, the Napoleonic occupation has had lasting benefits for Egyptology in the thorough survey carried out by the French engineers and scholars which was published as the *Description de l'Egypte* in 1828.

Nasser, Gamal Abdel (1918-70): One of the leaders of the 1952 Revolution, Gen. Nasser was President of Egypt between 1956 and his sudden death in 1970. He is chiefly remembered for his instigation of the High Dam Project (see **A-Z**), and for his central role in the Suez

Crisis of 1956 and the Six Day War with Israel in 1967. He is buried in Abbasseya in a tomb behind the mosque which bears his name.

Nefertari: The beloved chief wife of Ramesses II (see **A-Z**), who paid her the unique compliment of representing her on the same scale as himself on the temple he built for her at Abu Simbel (see **A-Z**). Her magnificent tomb in the Valley of the Queens (see **A-Z**) has recently been restored, and it is hoped that it will soon be open to the public.

Newspapers: Imported English-language newspapers and magazines are available from hotel bookshops and from stands in the street. In Cairo there is a good one next to Groppi's Café on Talaat Harb Sq.; in Luxor, try the station and the kiosk in front of the Tourist Bazaar. The daily English-language newspaper, the *Egyptian Gazette*, and the *Egyptian Mail* on Sat. cover international and domestic news, sports and local events as well as TV and radio programmes. Other English-language publications include current affairs and women's magazines. See **What's On**.

Nightlife: Cairo's best nightclubs are those attached to the international hotels; these usually have outdoor and indoor venues for the summer and winter respectively. They are very popular, and it is best to reserve a table, particularly for Thu. or Fri. nights. Shows normally include a belly dancer, an Arabic singer and folkloric dancers, and there may also be an international-style floor show, Arabic comedian or variety act: there are no risqué elements in Egyptian cabaret. Dress is formal and hours are late by European standards; diners normally eat around 2400, and the show starts in the early hours. In response to demand from tourists, however, some clubs now have early supper shows finishing around 2200. Some clubs charge an admission fee which includes dinner; others have a minimum charge. Minimum age is 21. During Ramadan (see **A-Z**) all nightclubs are closed, but some hotels have folklore shows.

Both Cairo and Luxor have some excellent and sophisticated discos, with state-of-the-art sound and lighting systems. These are usually attached to the big hotels. To eliminate undesirable elements, reputable discos always have a couples-only policy; don't be discouraged, as respectable-looking groups and singles will be admitted. Most good discos also have a minimum charge and require smart dress; jeans are not acceptable. Where alcohol is served, there is a minimum age limit of 21; some of the larger Cairo discos open up for teenagers in the afternoon.

Open only to non-Egyptians, casinos are open around the clock. Admission is by passport identification and play is in US dollars. Some casinos provide players with free drinks.

Cairo's bars are popular meeting places, often frequented by businessmen. Most have a minimum charge, and where there is live music, an entertainment tax is added to the bill. There is also the normal service tax of 12.5%. The clientele is predominantly male; lone women may feel uncomfortable in bars. Again the minimum age limit for casinos and bars is 21. See **CAIRO-BARS, NIGHTLIFE 1 & 2, LUXOR-NIGHTLIFE**.

Nile: The Greek historian Herodotus referred to Egypt as 'the gift of the river', because of the water and rich silt that made cultivation possible. 6695 km in length, the Nile is the world's longest river. It has two sources, the White Nile, which flows from Lake Victoria, and the Blue Nile, which carries seasonal runoff waters from the Ethiopian plateau and formerly caused the annual inundation. This is now controlled by

the High Dam (see **A-Z**) which regulates the flow to allow for perennial irrigation and electricity generation.

Nile Cruises: *The* most relaxing way to enjoy the beautiful Nile scenery. Long and short cruises are available to suit all tastes and pockets. Book in advance with a travel agent, or with a cruise company like TransEgypt Travel, 37 Kasr el Nil St, Central Cairo, tel: 3924313.

Nilometer: Before the Nile was dammed, the level of its annual inundation directly affected Egypt's agricultural productivity. It was therefore necessary to accurately measure the rise of the water, and special chambers called Nilometers were constructed to do this. There are many examples of Pharaonic Nilometers; perhaps the best known is on Elephantine Island in Aswan (see **LUXOR-EXCURSION 2**). Cairo's Nilometer (see **CAIRO-BUILDINGS & MONUMENTS 2**) dates from AD 861, and is the city's oldest Islamic monument.

Old Cairo: Masr el Qadima. Site of the first settlement in the Cairo area, this traditionally Christian quarter is built on and around the ruins of the Fortress of Babylon (see **A-Z**), parts of which are still visible. Other sights include the Coptic Museum (see **A-Z**), the Ben Ezra Synagogue (see **A-Z**) and several important early churches such as St. Sergius (see **A-Z**) and St. Barbara (see **A-Z**).

Opening Times: Opening times in Egypt are flexible: hours vary between summer and winter, and are different again during Ramadan (see **A-Z**), though some shops, restaurants, banks and offices have adapted to meet the needs of tourists and the international business community. Therefore, the times below should be treated as general guidelines.
Shops – 0900-1300, 1700-2000 summer; 1000-1800 winter. Closed Sun. and public holidays.
Banks – 0830-1330. Closed Fri., Sun. and public holidays.
Post Offices – 0830-1500. Closed Fri.

Government Offices – 0800-1400. Closed Fri., Sat. and public holidays.
Offices – 0900-1300, 1700-1900 summer; 0800-1400 winter. Closed Fri. and public holidays.
Large Museums – 0900-1600 Sat.-Thu.; 0900-1100, 1300-1600 Fri.
Small Museums – 0900-1400. Closed Fri. or Mon. and public holidays.
Archaeological Sites – 0600-1800 summer; 0600-1600 winter.

Opera House: Cairo's newest landmark, the Opera House was built with Japanese cooperation. Replacing the old Opera House, which was destroyed by fire in 1971, the new complex opened in 1988 and includes three concert halls plus exhibition and conference facilities. It presents a varied programme of cultural events: see the local press for details. See **CAIRO-BUILDINGS & MONUMENTS 3**, **Folk Music & Dance**, **Theatre**.

Ottomans: After Egypt fell to the Ottoman Turks in 1517, it was ruled by a series of viceroys appointed from Istanbul. In practice, however, power largely remained in the hands of the unscrupulous Mamluks (see **A-Z**), with the result that the country went into decline, and was too weak to resist the Napoleonic invasion of 1798. Ottoman monuments in Cairo include the Bayt el Suhaymi (see **A-Z**), the Gayer-Anderson Museum (see **CAIRO-MUSE-UMS 1**) and the Sulayman Pasha Mosque in the Citadel (see **A-Z**).

Papyrus: In ancient Egypt the stems of the plant *Cyperus Papyrus* were used to manufacture the forerunner of modern paper. Both the plant and the technique were lost to Egypt until a retired diplomat called Dr Ragab successfully applied himself to the problem. His Papyrus Institutes, on houseboats at Nile St in Cairo and the Corniche in Luxor, are good places to see the manufacture of papyrus. There are numerous similar establishments all over Cairo, particularly in the Pyramids area. Colourful painted papyrus is a popular souvenir, light and easily packed, but it is important to shop around before buying. Stories that cheap papyrus is made from banana leaves are untrue, but do compare quality. See **Best Buys**.

Parks & Gardens: Apart from the Botanical Gardens (see **A-Z**), the Zoo (see **A-Z**) and the Aquarium (see **CAIRO-CHILDREN**), Cairo has many attractive parks including the Andalus and Nile gardens opposite the El Borg Hotel in Zamalek. Tahrir Gardens, at the tip of Gezira Island, contain a collection of sculptures by Mahmud Mukhtar (see **A-Z**).

Passports & Customs: A visa is required for entry to Egypt; this can be obtained in advance from an Egyptian consulate or on arrival at the airport and is valid for one month. It must be paid for in hard currency – only cash is accepted. If you are arriving from an area infected with cholera or yellow fever, you must produce a WHO International Certificate of Vaccination confirming that you have been inoculated. At customs you should complete a Currency Declaration Form and declare any valuable possessions to avoid possible confiscation or duty on departure. All non-Egyptians are required to register with the authorities within seven days of arrival in Egypt, and within 24 hr of each change of address. This is normally done automatically by hotels, but if you must do it yourself, simply take your passport to the local police station or to the nearest registration office. In Cairo this is at the Mugamaa building in Tahrir Sq. and in Luxor on the Corniche next to the PLM Etap Hotel. Visas can also be renewed at the Mugamaa building in Tahrir Sq. You will need your passport, currency receipts to the value of US$150 for each month's required extension and two photos; there is a small fee for this service. See **Customs Allowances**.

Petrol: Petrol stations and repair shops can be found everywhere in Cairo, and in Luxor near the station and on the airport road. Both oil and petrol are sold by the litre. Petrol (*benzeen*) comes in two grades, super (90 octane) and regular (80 octane). It is usual to tip the attendant. See **Driving**.

Police: In the cities, police (*bulees*) wear black and white in winter and white in summer; in rural areas they wear khaki. Tourist police, who usually speak some English, are on duty at tourist sites and hotels and can be identified by their special armbands. See **Crime & Theft**, **Emergency Numbers**.

Post Offices: Post offices (*bustaat*) can be identified by a sign with a white dove holding a letter on a red, black and white background. Postboxes are colour-coded – overseas airmail goes in the blue box. Main post offices are in Cairo at Ataba Sq., Central Cairo (24 hr, except Fri.), and in Luxor at Station St (0930-1300). Stamps may also be bought at shops and hotels: a small commission is normally charged.

Ptolemies: Following the death of Alexander the Great (see **A-Z**), the rule of Egypt passed into the hands of its governor, Ptolemy Soter, who went on to found his own royal dynasty. The Ptolemies perpetuated the old Egyptian beliefs regarding kingship and religion, and to this end built many temples in the Egyptian style, notably those at Dendera (see **A-Z**), Edfu (see **A-Z**) and Kom Ombo (see **A-Z**). The last of the Ptolemaic line was Cleopatra the Great (see **A-Z**), whose defeat at the Battle of Actium led to Rome's annexation of Egypt.

Public Holidays: On public holidays all banks, government offices and businesses close. In addition to religious holidays (see **Festivals & Calendars**), the following secular holidays are observed:
Mon. after Coptic Easter (Shamm el Nessim – Spring Festival); 25 April (Sinai Liberation Day); 1 May (Labour Day); 23 July (Revolution Day); 6 Oct. (Armed Forces Day).

Pyramids: El Ahram. The significance of these royal tombs is still disputed, but the pyramid form seems to be connected with the cult of the sun god Re which was predominant during the Old Kingdom. The first pyramid was the Step Pyramid, built for King Djoser around 2700 BC. It seems to have been conceived as a series of mastabas (see **A-Z**), one on top of the other, as if to form a staircase for the king's soul to ascend to the sky. By the time that the Great Pyramid (see **A-Z**) was built, the true pyramid shape had evolved, and the conventional pyramid complex comprising pyramid, mortuary temple, causeway and valley temple had been established. From the late Old Kingdom, pyramid building went into decline, as can be seen from the Fifth and Sixth Dynasty pyramids at Sakkara (see **A-Z**), and by the New Kingdom it had ceased altogether. See **CAIRO-BUILDINGS & MONUMENTS 1, WALK 1**.

Pyramids, Giza

Qaitbey Complex: The complex of Sultan el Ashraf Qaitbey (1468-96) is perhaps the finest example of Islamic architecture in Cairo. Located in the Northern Cemetery (see **City of the Dead**) it is not easy to find, but is certainly worth the effort when you arrive. Built 1472-74, and richly decorated in the style of the late Mamluk (see **A-Z**) period, it comprises a *sabil* (public water fountain), *kuttab* (Qur'anic school) and madrasa (see **A-Z**) in addition to the Sultan's mausoleum. It is possible to climb up onto the roof in order to examine the ornately-carved dome and minaret in close-up, and to take in the panoramic view of the cemeteries.

Qalawun Complex: Located close to the Khan el Khalili bazaar (see **A-Z**), the complex of Sultan el Mansur Qalawun (1279-90) comprises a hospital, madrasa (see **A-Z**) and mausoleum and is a good example of early Mamluk (see **A-Z**) architecture. Built 1284-85, the mausoleum in particular is worth seeing for the richness and variety of its decoration which includes stained glass, inlaid stone and stucco work. See **CAIRO-BUILDINGS & MONUMENTS 2**.

Railways: There is a cheap and convenient railway system which links Cairo with Alexandria, Luxor and Upper Egypt. There are three classes of accommodation: third is very basic indeed, first is air condi-tioned and comfortable. Trains to Alexandria run approximately every hour throughout the day; the journey takes about 3 hr. There are sever-al trains a day between Cairo and Luxor, with a journey time of about 8 hr. First class accommodation is limited, so it is essential to book seats in advance; this can be done at Ramses station in Cairo or Luxor sta-tion, up to a week ahead. Students get a reduction of 50% on their fares on production of an International Student Card. There is also a comfort-able overnight sleeper service between Cairo and Luxor; there are two trains nightly and again it is necessary to make advance reservations. This can be done via a travel agent or directly with Compagnie Internationale des Wagons Lits Egypte, 48 Giza St, Giza, tel: 3487354, 9 Menes St, Heliopolis, tel: 2908802, and the Old Winter Palace build-ing, Luxor, tel: 382317. There are no student reductions on sleeper fares.

Ramadan: During the month of Ramadan, which generally falls in Feb. or Mar., in which the Holy Qur'an was revealed to the Prophet Muhammad, all healthy adult Muslims are required to fast. The fast, which involves abstinence from all eating, drinking, smoking and sex, lasts from dawn until dusk, when the breaking of the fast is announced by a cannon shot from the Citadel (see **A-Z**). Although fasting can be hard, particularly in hot weather, most Egyptians, especially children, look forward to Ramadan as a time of great blessings and festivity. Working hours are short, with many shops and offices closed for most of the day. The night, however, is long, as family and friends pay social calls, men gather to gossip in the cafés and the TV shows blockbuster movies into the small hours. Tourism services are generally unaffected by Ramadan, though monuments open later and close earlier, and outside of tourist establishments it can be difficult to find restaurants or cafés open during the day. A bonus for women travellers is that sexual harassment is at a minimum during this time. See **Meal Times**.

Ramesses II (c.1279-1212 BC):
A giant in Egyptian history, the size of Ramesses II's achievements was matched by that of his monuments – and his ego. During his 67-year reign he consolidated Egypt's position in the Near East by repelling attempted invasions and by concluding a peace treaty with the Hittites. Under Ramesses' rule the economy flourished; this enabled him not only to complete many of his father Seti I's (see **A-Z**) monuments, but to erect numerous grandiose buildings of his own, including the temples at Abu Simbel (see **A-Z**) and his mortuary temple, the Ramesseum (see **A-Z**). Devoted to his family, especially his lovely wife Nefertari (see **A-Z**), he is said to have had 162 children: his son Merneptah, who succeeded him, may have been the pharaoh of the Exodus.

Ramesses III (c.1182-1151 BC): Ramesses III appears to have been obsessed with the achievements and reputation of his famous pre-decessor, Ramesses II (see **A-Z**), slavishly copying the style and layout of his monuments; his mortuary temple at Medinet Habu is almost a carbon copy of the Ramesseum (see **A-Z**). Like his forerunner, Ramesses was obliged to repel no fewer than three foreign invasions, but in this case, the expense of the campaigns together with his extravagant build-ing programme combined to empty the treasury and bring the country close to ruin. Ramesses died in the 31st year of his reign, in suspicious circumstances following the discovery of a murder conspiracy in his harem.

Ramesseum: Located on the West Bank at Luxor, the mortuary tem-ple of Ramesses II (see **A-Z**), though ruined, has great romantic appeal. Entry is via the second court, lined with colossal statues of Ramesses as the god Osiris, but even these are dwarfed by the fallen seated colossus on the left. Originally measuring 17 m in height, it was the inspiration for Shelley's poem *Ozymandias*. See **LUXOR-BUILDINGS & MONUMENTS 2.**

Religious Services: Muslim prayer times are announced daily in the media. Cairo's many churches serve all nationalities and denominations; services are announced monthly in *Cairo Today* magazine and every Sat. in the *Egyptian Mail*. In Luxor, Mass is celebrated daily at 1800 in French, Italian or Arabic at Holy Family Catholic Church in Karnak Temple St. Luxor also has a Free Methodist Church just off Cleopatra St, a Pentecostal Church in Hatshepsut St and a Protestant Evangelical Church in Karnak Temple St; enquire locally for service times.

Romans: Following their annexation of Egypt in 30 BC, the Romans set about restoring the country's economic stability – dependent on Egyptian grain, their chief interest was making the new province as productive as possible. To this end, they went to great lengths to keep the powerful priesthoods happy with tax exemptions, land grants and temple-building programmes: monuments dating from this period include the temples at Esna (see **A-Z**) and Philae (see **LUXOR-EXCURSION 2**) and the Fortress of Babylon (see **A-Z**) in Old Cairo.

St. Barbara's Church: Although there may have been a church on this site as early as the 4thC, the present building dates mainly from the 11thC. The main part is dedicated to St. Barbara, a young woman killed by her father for trying to convert him to Christianity. The fine sanctuary screen is made of wood inlaid with ivory and dates back to the 13thC. See **CAIRO-WALK 2**.

St. Catherine's Monastery: Built on the site of the Burning Bush where God spoke to Moses, and in the shadow of the mountain where the Ten Commandments were received, St. Catherine's Monastery has been a site of pilgrimage for many centuries. The present monastery, occupied by Greek Orthodox monks, dates from the 6thC and houses priceless collections of ancient manuscripts and icons; its setting in the barren Sinai desert is extremely dramatic. See **Monasteries**.

St. Sergius' Church: Dedicated to the Roman martyrs Sergius and Bacchus, this is one of Cairo's oldest churches, originally dating from the 5thC, though the present structure dates from the Fatimid (see **A-Z**) period. The oldest part of the building was constructed over the cave where the Holy Family are said to have stayed during the Flight into Egypt. Unfortunately this crypt can no longer be visited, as flooding caused by a rise in the water table has made it inaccessible. The church's many remarkable works of art include icons, wall paintings and mosaics, as well as an 8thC carving of the Last Supper. See **CAIRO-BUILDINGS & MONUMENTS 1, WALK 2**.

Sadat, Anwar el (1918-81): In 1971, Anwar el Sadat succeeded Gamal Abdel Nasser (see **A-Z**) as president of Egypt. One of the leaders of the 1952 Revolution, he expelled the Russian presence after the completion of the High Dam (see **A-Z**), but is best remembered for his role in the 1972 October War against Israel and the subsequent Camp David Agreement. Sadat was assassinated in 1981. He is buried beneath the Victory Memorial at Medinet Nasr, near Heliopolis.

SAK

Sakkara: As the necropolis of the Old Kingdom capital of Memphis (see **A-Z**), Sakkara is one of the most important archaeological sites in the whole of Egypt, and has funerary monuments which span more than 3000 years of history. Among the most notable are the Step Pyramid (the world's oldest stone monument), the Mastabas of the Nobles and the Serapeum. See **CAIRO-BUILDINGS & MONUMENTS 1, EXCURSION 1.**

Saladin (1137-1193): As a Kurd in the employ of the Fatimids (see **A-Z**), Salah el Din El Ayyubi nursed the ambition of returning Egypt to Sunni Islam. With the death of the last Fatimid Caliph in 1171 he seized the opportunity and had himself appointed ruler of Egypt and its then extensive territories. Better known in the West as Saladin, he went on to gain many famous victories against the Crusaders, and parts of his Citadel (see **A-Z**) in Cairo were built by Crusader prisoners. He was also responsible for introducing the madrasa (see **A-Z**) to Cairo. His descendants, the Ayyubids, went on to rule until 1250, when power passed to the Mamluks (see **A-Z**).

Seti I (1291-1278 BC): A victorious warrior and wise king, he initiated massive building programmes and paved the way for the successful reign of his son Ramesses II (see **A-Z**). His monuments include his temple at Abydos (see **A-Z**) and the Hypostyle Hall at Karnak (see **A-Z**). His magnificent tomb is the finest in the Valley of the Kings (see **A-Z**).

Shopping: There are some wonderful bargains to be had in Egypt, but always remember that there are some unscrupulous salesmen only interested in parting tourists from their money. To avoid being ripped off, take some time to check out the prices in local stores (where Egyptians shop) and learn to read prices written in Arabic. There are two kinds of place to shop in Egypt – regular, fixed-price stores and markets, where bargaining is the order of the day. Don't allow yourself to be pressured into buying something you don't want or paying more than you want to, and bear in mind that if you go shopping with a guide or tour leader prices will reflect the fact that they receive a commission on your purchases. Many Egyptian shops operate on the Continental system where you take a slip to the till to pay, and then take the receipt to the collection point to pick up your purchases. Some shops now accept major credit cards, but not hard currency; payment must be in Egyptian pounds.

Cairo has some good Western-style supermarkets, such as Alfa Market (see **CAIRO-SHOPPING 3**). Unfortunately, there is nothing comparable in Luxor, but a good general grocery store is Dalia Supermarket in Television St. See **CAIRO-SHOPPING 1-3**, **LUXOR-SHOPPING**, **Bargaining**, **Best Buys**, **Markets**.

Sound & Light Shows: Twice-nightly Sound and Light performances are held at the Pyramids and at Karnak; using dramatic musical and lighting effects, they relate episodes from Egyptian history and are an impressive way to experience the monuments. Organized tours are available, or you can make your own transport arrangements and buy tickets at the site. Remember to take a coat or blanket, as it can be cold at night.

Sphinx: A sphinx is a mythical creature which combines the body of a lion with the head of a king or queen, and represents the ruler as the incarnate sun god. The Great Sphinx at Giza represents King Chephren; carved from a limestone outcrop, the figure protects his mortuary complex. Between its paws is a stela of Tuthmosis IV relating how the Sphinx appeared to him in a dream, promising him the throne if he would clear the sand from its body. Naturally Tuthmosis obliged, and

the prophecy was fulfilled! See **CAIRO-BUILDINGS & MONUMENTS 1**,
WALK 1.

Suez Canal: Designed by French engineer Ferdinand de Lesseps and
opened in 1869, the Suez Canal revolutionized transport between
Europe and the East. Formerly under British control, it was nationalized
by Nasser (see **A-Z**) in 1956 and is now one of Egypt's main sources of
income.

Sultan Hassan Madrasa: Built 1356-63, the madrasa (see **A-Z**) of
Sultan Hassan is one of the masterpieces of Mamluk (see **A-Z**) architecture. Its most impressive feature is the huge courtyard surrounded by
four vast *liwans* or recesses once used for teaching the four rites of
Sunni Islam. Behind the eastern *liwan*, which also serves as the mosque
sanctuary, is the sultan's mausoleum with its ornate and colourful decoration. See **CAIRO-BUILDINGS & MONUMENTS 2**.

Swimming: Many major hotels and sporting clubs have swimming
pools which are available to non-residents/members on payment of a
small charge. It is important to avoid swimming in canals, as bilharzia
is prevalent, and swimming in the Nile is not recommended either.
When swimming around the Red Sea reefs, it is a good idea to wear
gym shoes or similar to avoid cuts from the coral. See **CAIRO-SPORTS &
ACTIVITIES, LUXOR-SPORTS & ACTIVITIES**.

Taxis: Cairo's taxis are black and white; they can either be hailed in
the street or picked up outside hotels, in which case you will pay more.
If you hail a cab in the street, it is usual for the driver to pick up other
passengers going in the same direction. Taxis do have meters, but they
are seldom operative; people pay what they feel is right. Tourists are
expected to pay more, but beware of unscrupulous drivers who try to
charge exorbitant amounts. Comfortable limousines are available at
hotels; more expensive than taxis, they have the advantage of having
fixed prices. You can use the limousine tariff as a gauge to taxi fares – a
taxi should cost about half as much. As a rule, taxi drivers only speak
Arabic, so get someone to write or explain your destination for you.

They also expect you to know where you are going, so check the district and find out a nearby landmark. In Luxor, taxis can be found outside all large hotels, or they can be hailed in the street. They do not have meters, but drivers must be licensed. The official tariff for taxi fares is available from the tourist information office; it is well worth consulting as drivers frequently attempt to overcharge. Many hotels also offer price guidelines. Any problem with a taxi driver should be reported to the tourist police, quoting the driver's number. Service taxis are shared taxis which operate within Cairo and between cities. An extremely cheap way to travel, they operate on a first-come first-served basis and leave when all seats have been purchased. In Cairo, there are several stations for various destinations in the Ramses Sq. area; in Luxor, the station is on Karnak Temple St, just before the YMCA camp. See **Tipping**.

Telephones & Telegrams: International direct lines are available from both Cairo and Luxor, and major hotels in both cities offer telephone, telex and fax facilities to residents and non-residents alike. Cheaper but less convenient are the Central Telephone and Telegraph offices, open 24 hr. In Cairo these are at 8 Adly St, 26 Ramses St and Tahrir Sq., all in Central Cairo, and in Luxor at Karnak Temple St behind the Savoy Hotel. Also in Luxor, the Winter Palace Telephone, Telegram and Telex Office, Old Winter Palace building, Corniche el Nil, tel: 383156, is open 0800-2130. There may be delays in obtaining both national and international lines.
International codes – UK 44, Eire 353, USA 1, Canada 1, Australia 61, New Zealand 64.
Cairo telephone numbers may change without notice, as new numbers are currently being allocated. Some numbers beginning with 74, 75 and 77 will change; substitute 392 for numbers beginning with 74 and 77, and 393 for numbers beginning with 75.

Television & Radio: Radio Cairo's European Service on 557AM and 95FM is on the air 0700-2400 with music and general entertainment in several European languages. English news is at 0730, 1430 and 2000. Other stations include BBC World Service on 639 and 1325

KHz and Voice of America on several frequencies including 7200 and 9700 KHz; both stations broadcast news on the hour. There are three TV channels: Channel 1 (1530-2400) and Channel 2 (1500-2400 daily, plus 1000-1200 Fri. and Sun.) have quite a few English-language films and serials. Channel 3 (1700-2100) is Cairo's local station, broadcasting in Arabic only. English news is on Channel 2 at 2000. TV and radio programme details are published daily in the *Egyptian Gazette*.

Temple of Hatshepsut: Built for the female pharaoh Hatshepsut (see **A-Z**) in the 16thC BC, the temple at Deir el Bahari, with its three colonnaded terraces, presents a striking aspect – particularly when it is illuminated at night. It was originally set among gardens, with pools and avenues of trees; some of the roots are visible in pits near the entrance. Of particular interest are the reliefs on the second terrace which tell the story of Hatshepsut's divine birth and of her trade expedition to the exotic land of Punt. See **LUXOR-BUILDINGS & MONUMENTS 1**.

Temple of Ramesses III: Dating from the 12thC BC, the mortuary temple of Ramesses III (see **A-Z**) at Medinet Habu has many interesting and unusual features. Largely modelled on the Ramesseum (see **A-Z**), here the sunk reliefs are taken a stage further, with inscriptions carved 10 cm deep. The crenellated entrance gate is thought to represent the fortresses encountered during his Syrian campaigns, and there are numerous battle scenes carved both on the outer walls and in the first court of the temple itself. Here there is also a 'Window of Appearances' where the king would show himself to the assembled company; it is connected to the palace buildings behind. The colossal mummiform figures of the king are reminiscent of those in his small temple at Karnak (see **A-Z**). The reliefs in the second court and the rooms beyond are concerned with the religious ritual of the temple; there are some interesting scenes of the procession of the fertility god Min, and, at the rear of the temple, a suite of rooms dedicated to the cult of Osiris. See **LUXOR-BUILDINGS & MONUMENTS 1**.

Temples: Egyptian temples were built on a standard pattern comprising a pylon or ornamental gateway, an open court, a hypostyle or columned hall and a sanctuary surrounded by small chapels and storerooms. Called 'Gods' Houses', it was believed that the deity was actually present to receive the mountains of offerings that were presented in the daily rituals to ensure the continued order of the universe. Temples were frequently enlarged and elaborated by succeeding generations of rulers, and it is rare for a temple to date to a single reign.

Theatre: In addition to the venues below, there are frequent presentations of music, dance and theatre by large hotels and cultural organizations such as the British Council; check the events columns in the local press.
Balloon Theatre: On the corner of Nile St and 26 July St, Agouza, tel: 3471718. Look out for folk dance performances by the National Troupe and Reda Troupe held regularly at this theatre.
Opera House (see **A-Z**): tel: 3420598. Huge new complex includes three concert halls and presents a varied programme of cultural events including modern dance and classical ballet, opera, jazz and Arabic

music, and international folk music and dance. Check press for details of the current programme. Men must wear a suit and tie for performances in the main hall. See **Newspapers**, **What's On**.

Thebes: Known to the ancient Egyptians as Waset, Thebes was the Greek name for the area now known as Luxor.

Time Differences: Winter time in Egypt is 2 hr ahead of GMT; in summer the clocks go forward 1 hr.

Tipping: Tipping is a way of life in Egypt; in many occupations wages are so low that people are dependent on tips for their living. If you accept any service, however small, you will be expected to tip for it; this includes porters, lavatory attendants, etc. On tours, it is usual to tip the guide, driver and tour leader, and it is customary to add a small tip when paying boatmen, carriage drivers, etc. In restaurants, although a service tax is included, it is usual to add something for the waiters. Try not to become irritated by the constant demands for money, but on the other hand, never allow yourself to be pressured into tipping more than you want to. A shortage of change is often a problem, so make sure when changing money to get as many small notes and coins as you can. Tour company representatives can offer guidelines as to appropriate amounts for tips.

Toilets: Public toilets are few and far between and facilities are very basic indeed: always carry tissues and wet wipes with you. It is quite acceptable to go into a hotel and use the toilets there for free, but if you use the facilities in a café you should at least buy a drink. Lavatory attendants always expect a small tip.

Tombs of the Nobles: The rock-cut Tombs of the Nobles at Luxor are among the most popular sights on the West Bank. Belonging to priests and courtiers who hoped to resume their privileged life style after death, their bright colours and vivid daily-life scenes seem to bring the past alive. Particularly interesting are those of Rekhmire, with its scenes of the temple workshops at Karnak, Sennefer with undulating

A–Z

grape vines on the ceiling, Nakht for its agricultural scenes and Ramose for its fine reliefs. Most organized tours of the West Bank visit some of these. See **LUXOR-BUILDINGS & MONUMENTS 1**.

Tourist Information: Main Tourist Information offices are located at 5 Adly St, Central Cairo, tel: 3936160, and at the Tourist Bazaar, Corniche el Nil, Luxor, tel: 382215. Tour company representatives and hotel reception staff are also good sources of local information. *Cairo Today* magazine has excellent sightseeing and events listings. See **Accommodation**, **Guides**, **Tours**, **What's On**.

Tours: Though more expensive than going it alone, organized excursions are an excellent option for visitors with limited time at their disposal. In Cairo itself, half-day tours of Old Cairo, the Egyptian Museum and Islamic Cairo provide good orientation, while a full-day visit to the Old Kingdom sites of Memphis, Sakkara and Giza is rightly on every tourist itinerary. Some interesting destinations further afield include Alexandria, the monasteries of Wadi Natrun and the Suez Canal, all

accessible by road. Air excursions extend the possibilities still further, with trips to Luxor, Aswan, Abu Simbel and St. Catherine's Monastery. Besides a choice of tours of the monuments of the East and West banks, visitors based in Luxor have the chance to visit a number of other ancient sites, including the temples of Abydos, Dendera, Esna, Edfu and Kom Ombo. A day trip to Aswan is a popular choice, as are the air excursions to Cairo and Abu Simbel. Other attractive options include short Nile cruises, or visits to Hurghada on the Red Sea coast. Excursions can be booked either through your tour company representative or travel agents, many of whom have desks in hotels. Prices and departure times will vary. See **Guides, Tourist Information**.

Transport: See **Airports, Boats, Buses, Calèches, Feluccas, Metro, Railways, Taxis**.

Traveller's Cheques: See **Money**.

Tutankhamun (c.1334-1325 BC): The son of the heretic king Akhenaten (see **A-Z**) by a minor queen, the young prince, originally named Tutankhaten, succeeded his father on the throne of Egypt at the age of nine but died in mysterious circumstances only nine years later. As Tutankhamun, he restored the cult of the Theban god Amun, but nonetheless his name was removed from the records and his existence remained unknown until the discovery of some objects from his tomb in the Valley of the Kings (see **A-Z**). It was these that led Howard Carter to find the tomb itself in 1922; Tutankhamun's body still rests there in his sarcophagus. Although the tomb is currently closed to the public, its famous treasures are housed in the Egyptian Museum (see **A-Z**) in Cairo.

Tuthmosis III (c.1504-1450 BC): Egypt's great warrior pharaoh, Tuthmosis III, succeeded his stepmother, the female pharaoh Hatshepsut (see **A-Z**). His many military campaigns are commemorated at Karnak (see **A-Z**), but a more sensitive nature is indicated in some of his other monuments; his tomb in the Valley of the Kings (see **A-Z**) is particularly fine, and many beautiful sculptures date from his reign.

Upper & Lower Egypt: From ancient times, the Egyptians have seen their country as comprising two distinct lands known as Upper and Lower Egypt. Upper Egypt – the Nile valley – was symbolized by the lotus flower, and Lower Egypt – the delta – by the papyrus plant.

Valley of the Kings: Biban el Molouk. Prompted by a desire for greater security and in response to the restricted space available in the Nile valley, the kings of the New Kingdom abandoned the idea of building pyramid tombs. Instead, they chose deep, rock-cut tombs hidden away in a remote valley on the West Bank of the river opposite their capital of Thebes. The tombs are painted with brightly-coloured mythological scenes intended to assist the king in his rebirth and future life among the gods. Particularly fine tombs are those of Tuthmosis III, Seti I, Ramesses III and Ramesses VI. See **LUXOR-BUILDINGS & MONUMENTS 1**.

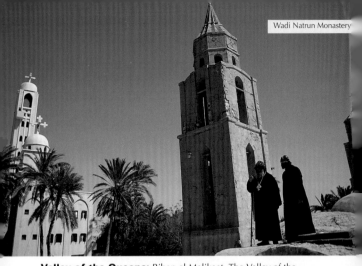

Valley of the Queens: Biban el Malikaat. The Valley of the Queens, a short distance from the Valley of the Kings (see **A-Z**), accommodates the tombs of New Kingdom queens and princes. Though smaller, they are similar in style to the kings' tombs and are also decorated with religious scenes. The finest belonged to Nefertari (see **A-Z**), wife of Ramesses II (see **A-Z**), and to Khaemwese and Amenhikhopshef, sons of Ramesses III (see **A-Z**). See **LUXOR-BUILDINGS & MONUMENTS 1**.

Wadi Natrun Monasteries: The Egyptian tradition of monasticism is extremely old, and the monasteries of the Wadi Natrun are some of the oldest functioning monasteries in the world. Situated in a desert depression 100 km northwest of Cairo, there are four monasteries which welcome visitors: the Monastery of St. Macarius, the Monastery of the Syrians, the Monastery of St. Bishoi and the Monastery of the Romans. See **Monasteries**.

Water: Municipal water in both Cairo and Luxor is chlorinated and therefore safe to drink, but because it could be contaminated before it reaches the tap, short-stay visitors are usually recommended to stick to bottled water. Under no circumstances should canal or river water be drunk.

What's On: *Cairo Today* is a monthly local interest magazine, invaluable for its extensive events listings; another useful listings booklet is *Cairo's*, also published monthly. A new bi-monthly magazine, *Places in Egypt*, gives in-depth coverage of tourism and leisure topics. See **Events, Newspapers**.

Wikalat el Ghuri: Dating from the Mamluk (see **A-Z**) period, a beautifully restored example of a medieval caravanserai, with shops on the ground floor and, upstairs, storerooms for merchandise and accommodation for the merchants. Today these rooms house the studios of artists and craftsmen. See **CAIRO-CRAFTS**.

Wissa Wassef School: Madrasat Wissa Wassef. Along with his friend Hassan Fathy (see **A-Z**), the architect Ramses Wissa Wassef was instrumental in the Egyptian arts and crafts revival of the 1930s and 40s. Like Fathy, he believed in the use of traditional Egyptian building techniques. The Wissa Wassef School at Harrania is an excellent example of his architectural style, and has won an Aga Khan Award. The school incorporates pottery and weaving workshops, and a museum of the world-famous Wissa Wassef tapestries. See **CAIRO-BUILDINGS & MONUMENTS 3, EXCURSION 1**.

Women: It is a regrettable fact that women visitors to Egypt have to face particular difficulties in terms of harassment. The root of the problem is that imported films and soap operas have done a good job in promoting an image of Western women as sexually promiscuous. Sadly, this now means that even simple friendly behaviour towards men must be curtailed, as it can easily be misinterpreted. Most harassment is verbal and best ignored, but a few simple precautions can help keep it to a minimum. Firstly, modest dress is essential – anything short, tight, low-cut or sleeveless will instantly attract the wrong kind of attention. Eye contact with men should be avoided (sunglasses are useful)